Confessions
of a
Depression Muralist

Confessions

of a

Depression

Muralist

FRANK W. LONG

UNIVERSITY OF MISSOURI PRESS

COLUMBIA AND LONDON

Library of Congress Cataloging-in-Publication Data

Long, Frank W.
    Confessions of a depression muralist / Frank W. Long.
        p.   cm.
    ISBN 0-8262-0994-7 (alk. paper)
    1. Long, Frank W.   2. Painters—United States—Biography.
I. Title.
ND237.L6994A2   1997
759.13—dc21
[B]   96-51958
                                                                    CIP

♾TM This paper meets the requirements of the
American National Standard for Permanence of Paper
for Printed Library Materials, Z39.48, 1984.

Designer: Susan Ferber
Typesetter: BOOKCOMP
Printer and binder: Thomson-Shore, Inc.
Typefaces: Bursten and Janson

Contents

Foreword

Sue Bridwell Beckham

ON A FAMILY VACATION IN 1982—a leisurely ramble through the Southeast, mostly to visit relatives, as I was just beginning research for my book on southern post office murals—we stopped to visit any murals that were less than fifty miles out of the way. Berea, Kentucky, was less than fifty miles from my aunt's house in Mt. Washington, it was on my list of mural locations, and I had forgotten about Kentucky roads—fifty miles on two-lane roads in the Appalachian foothills is a much greater undertaking than a hundred and fifty miles on any typical American highway.

Snaky roads, slow traffic, and breathtaking scenery aside, that particular mural side trip proved to be a cornerstone in my search for insight into southern Depression post office murals. The Berea mural was the first I had seen that both reflected genuine enthusiasm on the part of the artist and had generated community involvement that had persisted unabated for the intervening half century.

On the wall above the Berea postmaster's door is a five-by-twelve-foot painting of a crowd of people actively involved in celebration and commerce. In the confines of a concession stand, a quartet of jovial hosts serve their customers tall tales and comestibles with equal industry. Tucked into corners of the painting, couples engage in age-old rituals: an affectionate young woman entices a young man with his first taste of banana; another lass, who no doubt assumes the stomach and the heart to be interdependent, offers food from her picnic basket to a receptive lad; and a third young man serenades his lady fair with dulcimer accompaniment. In the busy middle ground and foreground, horse traders examine the teeth of a reluctant horse, oxen patiently pull a wagonload of women and children into the midst of the festivities, an apparent parson consults his book, and a dog expresses more than mild interest in a picnic hamper. In the background, peddlers hawk their wares and families eat sumptuous picnic lunches from blankets spread on the ground. Throughout the justifiably crowded scene, men shake hands on deals, women visit and flirt, children munch on special treats, and horses munch grass with equal enthusiasm. More than one hundred human figures and at least half again as many animals enjoy themselves in the mural. And the nearest ones occupy the foreground in such a way that the viewer cannot resist becoming part of the merrymaking. The whole tableau is rendered in vivid reds, blues, and yellows calculated to make postal patrons as pleased with their lot as the artist and his characters seem to be with theirs.

The postal worker on duty that day had no idea who had painted the picture, but he knew what it represented. It was *An Old-Time Berea Commencement*. Unlike most college towns, Berea and Berea College have no town-gown enmity—in earlier years hardly any separate being. Berea exists because the college exists, and each owes much of its well-being to the other. Virtually all Depression post office murals were illustrations, and the success of the mural in any given community depended in large part on whether the choice of illustration reflected the community's values and whether the rendering reflected the community's vision. Early Berea College commencement activities were, perhaps, more like annual fairs than academic rites. They provided excuses for myriad dwellers in the Appalachian foothills to come to town for fellowship and trade. And they were a time to celebrate the gifts of a college specifically established for their children and a bustling town ready to support their social and economic endeavors. The subject of the mural was all that a community could hope for, and as I was to learn, its artist had been an equally fortuitous choice.

We left the post office for the local tourist information center—appropriately situated in the community but staffed by the college. Like the postal worker, the college student staff could not name the artist, but they knew who could. "Dean" Smith, the octogenarian emeritus dean of the college, was still an important figure about town, and he had been there when the mural was painted. Dean Louis Smith turned out to be a longtime personal friend of the artist, and he directed me to Frank Long, a onetime Berea citizen who was now living in New Mexico and practicing lapidary as an art and a vocation.

My first correspondence with Long showed him to be that rarity among artists—an articulate writer with wide experience and wider interests who could look at his work in a broader context—and he was also willing to correspond about his work as a government muralist with an unknown woman who claimed she was writing a book.

Long's Berea mural turned out to be one of the most successful efforts of the New Deal program to decorate federal buildings with art that could be appreciated by the people. From the viewpoint of the art critic, the Berea mural was not Long's best mural work. The two monumental panels in the University of Kentucky Library are finer art, and the ten panels in his sequence for the Louisville post office more eloquently relate to the architectural spaces for which they were designed. But the Berea mural is his most successful. It is a fine work of art, it spoke and still speaks to its audience, and it represents government largesse at its best.

The mural in the Berea, Kentucky, post office was one of well over one thousand "post office murals" installed between 1935 and 1942 by the Treasury Section of Fine Arts—a New Deal agency that existed exclusively to commission professional artists to decorate new federal buildings with works of art that illustrated some aspect of the American scene or of American history.

Under the auspices of that agency and its predecessors, Long produced the two imposing University of Kentucky library panels, the ten-panel sequence for the majestic Louisville post office, three panels for the moderate-size post office in Hagerstown, Maryland, and single panels for four other small-town buildings. Seven buildings and nineteen panels may not seem to be many, but when one considers that the Section of Fine Arts existed for less than a decade, that artists were given from nine months to a year to complete a mural after designs were approved, and that many artists requested extensions of their original time allotment, nineteen panels by a single artist is impressive. In fact, Long created more mural panels for more Depression post offices than any other single artist.

But numbers do not represent Frank Long's most significant achievements in government service. What really makes his autobiography worth reading—besides the fact that Long spins his Depression-era life into a delightful yarn—is that in supplying those seven buildings with murals ranging from quite competent to very fine, Long experienced almost every type of conflict and almost every type of gratification the Section offered its artists. Long's memoir of painting post office murals for the Section provides the only account to date of that agency from the artist's perspective.

Long's emotions during his sojourn as a Section muralist ranged from elation over a job well done and satisfactorily completed to the

burnout that often drove artists from the Section after only two or
three projects. His relationship to his work and to the communities
for which he painted provides insight into the Section, its artists,
its activities, and its era from a perspective hitherto unavailable. Although Long is unlike many Section artists in that none of his murals
was negatively received by either the Section or the community in
which it was placed, he did run into enough difficulties related to
content, technique, and technology for his story to illustrate some of
the trials with which artists who painted murals for the government
and a community were faced. The response to Long's murals ranged
from quiet acceptance when he had no dealings with community
residents, to modest applause when he stayed several days in a community installing the mural and touching it up, to virtual jubilation
when he was one of few Section artists who designed and painted the
mural over the postmaster's door in his own hometown.

No artist ever built a reputation simply by painting murals for post
office lobbies. Many, however, felt that working for a government
agency that claimed to commission artists solely on the basis of skill
provided prestige that would boost their careers. Like others, Long
benefited from his government association. Because of his murals,
especially in Louisville and Lexington, he was asked to speak at a
number of functions (one suspects he was asked more often than
other artists because he was a good public speaker as well as an
accomplished artist and an articulate writer). And, undoubtedly,
because of those speaking engagements, art lovers and the media
paid more attention to his nonmural work than they otherwise might
have. While executing the government commissions that put food on
his table kept Long from wholehearted pursuit of his easel painting,
the visibility he gained through his connections with the Section of
Fine Arts furthered his reputation as an artist.

Frank Long's years as a Section artist were signal ones for his
career. During those years, he was Kentucky's foremost artist, he
was sublimely pleased with his situation in Berea, and he was satisfied
with his life. He had few problems with the Section that employed
him: he was adaptable, he caught on quickly to what was expected,
he delivered it, and he was forthright and articulate when he was
unhappy. He had few problems with communities because, although
he seldom had contact with them before he installed a mural, he

had a feel for the region. He was careful in selecting subject matter appropriate to the setting, and he was a very congenial fellow when he arrived to install his finished work. His artistic reach exceeded the purely local, in part because of his association with the Section. All of Long's murals survive in their original spaces, and each of them testifies to the success of the largest federal effort thus far to bring art to the people of the United States. These memoirs memorialize and elucidate that endeavor.

Confessions
of a
Depression Muralist

Prologue

NOW THAT IT IS FINISHED, I am suddenly surprised to
have written this book. As I think about it, it seems rather
strange that there should be enough serious interest today in the
murals I painted during the thirties and early forties to inspire anyone
with the idea that I should write a book about the experience. But it is
a fact that I did receive urging from a few people especially interested
in that unique period in American art during the Great Depression. I
find that a section of the public is now affected by a kind of nostalgia
for that period, even though they may have suffered the hardships
of that time along with everyone else.

It is not strange that the murals are receiving more attention now
than most of the other public works that were produced at that time;
they attracted more attention then too, because they were highly
visible and well publicized. It is fortunate indeed that so many murals
still exist in good condition today that a new assessment of their
importance can be made.

Comparatively recently, some reputable art critics have claimed
the discovery of greater artistic merit in these works than they were
credited with at the time. Right or wrong, this assessment has, of
course, helped to stimulate the renaissance of interest. Many among
the general public for whom these works have great appeal would
feel vindicated in their judgment if some real aesthetic significance
could now be found in the murals of this brief period of American art.

It is the murals that have attracted the most attention to my own
work during that time. I am not happy that this is the case, because
I have never considered myself a muralist by either accomplishment
or inclination. I cannot agree with the critics who find a great deal
to praise in the depression murals, including my own. The quality
on the whole is naturally very uneven. Mine were perhaps as good
as some, but undoubtedly inferior to others. But what I or the critics
think will not affect the ultimate critical judgment that only time can
establish. I only hope that my worth as an artist will be based on my
easel paintings rather than the murals, which do not represent the
best utilization of my talent.

It seems that everyone who remembers the government-subsidized murals today is convinced they were all done under the WPA (Works Progress Administration). Publicity for projects other than those of the WPA was scarce. The public was never made fully aware of the earlier PWAP (Public Works of Art Projects) or of the later Section of Fine Arts program under the Department of the Treasury. Actually, although some murals were by WPA artists, most were commissioned by the Section of Fine Arts, which functioned in an entirely different manner. Since all my murals, except the first, which I painted for the PWAP, were done for the Section of Fine Arts, I shall explain in my narrative the differences that existed in the methods of operation between these other art programs and the WPA.

Apparently most of the murals that graced the walls of government buildings remain in place. Surprisingly, it seems that over the years several of the communities where these murals were placed have become attached to them, even though many were hostile at first. In some communities where the government has decided to remove an old post office and replace it with a new one, efforts have been launched to persuade the government to move the murals to the new location. In cases where a mural has deteriorated, a request is often made that it be restored for the new building. To this extent, it is clear that murals have become real cultural assets to such communities, regardless of their merit as works of art. This was a result that the Section of Fine Arts tried so hard to achieve.

At the same time, those who formulated the program and persuaded the government to implement it visualized it as an opportunity to develop a truly American school of painting. Perhaps unfortunately, I could not be enthusiastic about this approach. I had to doubt that any movement based on a credo of prescribed chauvinism could produce art of significant artistic quality. Then too, the indirect, drawn-out process of creating a commissioned mural was very much at variance with my own approach to painting. At their best, my methods were spontaneous to a high degree. The only spontaneity possible in the creation of a mural under the circumstances imposed by the Section tended to be exhausted in the preparation of the initial sketch for approval. From there on, the completion of the mural became largely a mechanical task of faithfully reproducing the sketch to a larger scale. An artist of my temperament tends to rebel against what he sees as merely repeating the original conception, already fully realized in the approved design.

This being true, one may very well ask how I tolerated spending so much time and energy in the field of mural painting. Quite simply, the compelling motive was financial. This I know was true of many, if not most, of the artists engaged in the Section's mural program. They felt very much as I did about mural painting, but the prevailing economic conditions forced a reluctant retreat from artistic principles. This may not have been quite the same as giving in to the lure of the financial rewards possible in commercial art in normal times, but to me it was uncomfortably close.

Although in this account I shall describe my experience in painting each of the murals, the mural in the post office at Berea, Kentucky, will receive the most attention. There is good reason for this. Berea had become my home several years before I painted the mural there, and it was there that the other government murals were painted before being transferred to their permanent locations. Berea was the center of my life as an artist. The commission to do the Berea mural was perhaps the high point of my career as a muralist. In my opinion it was not my best mural, but it was certainly the most successful as far as the public was concerned. This mural is, of course, an illustration, as were most if not all of the Section's murals. As such, it cannot be considered a high form of creative art, perhaps; but it is precisely because it is an illustration of a long-established traditional event that the mural was, and still is, so popular.

Some researchers have claimed that this was the only small-town commission awarded by the Section on the basis of a competition to a local resident. This is almost certainly true because professional artists did not live in the small towns to which the Section murals were often allocated. "Local" competitions were in fact statewide and drew entrants from the larger cities where most artists lived, seeking a wider audience for their talents and greater patronage opportunities. Obviously, being intimately familiar with the setting and the community is a distinct advantage when designing a public mural for any particular location. In the Berea case, I was a resident there almost by accident, because the mural I had painted for the PWAP in Lexington, only forty miles away, had caused me to locate there.

Although this narrative is primarily concerned with describing my work and experiences as a muralist, it necessarily deals intimately with the life of the Berea community during the period it covers. Even though some of the passages may sound like fiction, I have made every effort to remain strictly factual in their narration. However, in some instances, the names of individuals have been changed. This has not been due to fear of prosecution for libel, but to avoid any possible embarrassment to living persons or the relatives of deceased persons who may be discussed or quoted. I am well aware of how easily even the most innocent description of local personalities and their peculiarities may be misinterpreted as ridicule.

One of the reasons, perhaps the principal one, for my having found Berea so compatible was my genuine interest in the people. They are of the same stock as the people I had become intimately acquainted with as a youth in the Great Smoky Mountains of my native Tennessee. They are the descendants of the first settlers of the Appalachian Mountain region: the English, Irish, and Scottish who emigrated to escape discrimination and harsh economic conditions during the reign of the British King James I. They still retain much of their original culture, including peculiarities of customs and speech.

One characteristic I found surprising and of special interest to me is their superlative ability to express themselves with great accuracy and effect in spite of a severely limited vocabulary. This seems to be an almost universal talent among them. In this connection, when quoting, I have tried to render faithfully the common speech, which differs so radically in its use of grammar and pronunciation from that found in most other American communities. But converting into print the unusual accents and intonations that characterize any vernacular can never be completely successful. I fear that my efforts may seem convincing only to those who are well acquainted with the speech itself, and they may very well find my interpretations far from perfect.

One of the most striking qualities of personality I noted among those I got to know was their strong individualism. Everyone seemed to have an original personality. This resulted in an astonishing number of local "characters," an anomaly noted by other observers as well. I have often heard it said that Madison County, Kentucky, the Berea locale, has more "characters" per square mile than any other place on earth. I have tried to describe my impressions of some of these individuals as faithfully as possible because I believe they had some effect, either subtle or pronounced, on both my painting and the life I led during that most interesting period.

The question of why I have spent so much time and effort on this book continues to occur to me. Reasons given by those who have wanted to see it materialize are that it is needed to correct the prevalent misunderstandings about the murals of the depression period; that there is a new and lively rebirth of interest among art lovers and art historians in the aesthetic quality of works created under government subsidy at that time; that there has been no comparable statement by any artist who was engaged in the program concerning what his participation meant to him as a struggling artist; and that such a book if capably written could have a strong appeal as both information and entertainment. It could tell a significant story through the humor and color of its unusual setting and personalities. These have been convincing arguments, but the most persuasive factor for writing the book has been the amount of enjoyment I myself discovered when I tentatively wrote the first two chapters.

I suppose the question of whether I might not have spent the time and effort more effectively, and to better purpose, in some form of expression in which I have more talent than in writing will remain. This can only be decided by comparing this effort with any works I may be able to create in the remaining years of my life.

A word about the title of this book—it may be misleading. If readers expect to be entertained by a revelation of scandalous, immoral escapades they will be disappointed. On the other hand, "Confessions" is appropriate enough to describe an account that deals frankly and honestly with my behavior, including mistakes I have made, during my career as a rather reluctant muralist.

CHAPTER 1
A Portrait Commission
Saves the Day

I HAVE TO SAY THAT IN ALL MY THINKING about painting as a career, I never anticipated that mural painting would be a part of it. Certainly, I never considered mural painting during my early studies of art in Chicago, Philadelphia, and Paris. It is possible that I believed such large-scale work was beyond my ability. I also may have thought that mural commissions would be highly unlikely for a beginning painter, even though one might become qualified through special study and training in that field.

In the schools I attended I don't believe the subject was ever taught as a part of the curriculum. But I do recall that at the Chicago Art Institute some of the advanced students worked as apprentices for John Norton, a well-known Chicago muralist of the time. Apparently there was some arrangement between Norton and the Institute. Since I was not in the advanced classes, having studied at the school for only two years, I would not have been eligible even if I had been interested. It seems rather strange to me now that while studying in France and viewing some of the splendid murals there I was never inspired with the thought that I might ultimately participate as a professional in this field. Unaccountably, I seem to have been afflicted with a kind of unconscious indifference. Now, after having been led by unforeseen circumstances to spend a great deal of my time as a muralist, I can clearly see the causes of my apathy. It was almost by accident that I finally became a painter of murals.

When I returned to the States from Europe early in 1929, the Great Depression was just getting under way. It was the worst possible time for an artist to think of trying to start a career. In Chicago, during the few months before the stock market crash, I managed to exist by several expedients. I found some work designing the icing decorations for wedding, birthday, and other special cakes, which were then executed by a caterer's pastry chefs; I also worked for an hour and a half each day as a busboy in a cafeteria in return for my meals. In addition, my ever-supportive parents came to my assistance during the leanest periods, although I knew they could hardly afford it.

In spite of the struggle, I managed somehow to continue painting during these hard times, and at last the tide seemed to turn. Another artist, a friend, introduced me to the director of the Walden-Dudensing Gallery, which had opened a short time before in the Drake Hotel on the lakeshore, a rather swanky setting. He came to my studio to see my work and was obviously impressed with what he saw. He offered me a one-man show for a couple of months in the spring of 1931. I was both surprised and elated. I spent every available hour on new work I hoped to have ready to exhibit, and I considered the result a good representation of my ability. The show looked very good when hung. The director, Mr. Manning, was very pleased with it and had a well-designed catalog printed. This was my first public exposure of any kind. Unfortunately, but no doubt predictably, not a single work was sold, not even a drawing! At the time, I considered this at least a minor tragedy.

Of course my failure could hardly have had anything to do with Mr. Dudensing's suicide a short time later. That was a result of the Wall Street crash, and his means of escape was one that became popular among previously wealthy businessmen at that time. The failure of the stock market also ushered in a period of desperation for many others who were barely making a living before it occurred, but being inured to financial hardship, few in that class resorted to self-destruction as a solution. For me, just as it seemed I had hit rock-bottom, Mr. Curt Teich appeared. Unknown to me, he was the owner of Curt Teich Lithograph Company, then the largest producer of colored picture postcards in the country.

As I remember it, it was on a bleak morning in October while I was gazing rather disconsolately out of my studio window that a long black chauffeured limousine came into view and pulled up to the curb across the street. This was on Rush Street in what was called Towertown—Chicago's equivalent of New York's Greenwich Village, a haven of artists, musicians, poets, art students, dilettantes, impostors, would-be artists, and assorted hangers-on. It was given that name because it was a neighborhood of several streets near the old Water Tower on Michigan Boulevard in Chicago's "near north side." I lived there in a large rented room and bath that served as a studio for both myself and Vincent Ripley, a friend from my student days at the Art Institute. The long black car with chauffeur was not unusual in this neighborhood where there were several excellent restaurants and more than one speakeasy (Prohibition was then in force), but when a portly middle-aged man got out, looked at the house numbers, and came directly across the street, I was curious. I entered the below-street-level vestibule of my building; after a moment, to my surprise, my bell rang. When I answered, a voice with a heavy German accent identified Curt Teich. He said he would like to talk with me about something he thought I might be interested in. With considerable wonder, I invited him to come up and unlocked the vestibule door.

When he was comfortably seated he began by introducing himself and saying he had recently been in Lexington, Kentucky, where he was introduced to my father, also a painter, by a friend of his who lived in that city. He said he had had the pleasure of visiting my parents in their home and had seen there a portrait of my father, painted by me. He professed great admiration for the picture, particularly the style in which it was done, coupled with the fact that he thought it a remarkable likeness. He said, in his thick German syllables, "Meester Long, I dell you vhy I am goming to zee you. I haf been dinking mebby I can get you to baint un bortrait of mine vife the zame vay you binted your fodder—zo beautiful mit ze liddle spots of color all over."

I had painted the portrait of my father when I was home on vacation from the Pennsylvania Academy of Fine Art in Philadelphia. We had been studying the impressionist and pointillist techniques of the French masters, and the painting had come off fairly well as a demonstration of painting with spots of pure primary and secondary colors placed side by side to create shades of tertiary and quaternary hues when viewed at a distance. This produced a vibration of the colors by mixing their optical images rather than the pigments themselves. I was surprised that this innovative technique would impress someone who I suspected was not familiar with its origin. He went on, "Of gourse I know you haf not zeen mine vife und you don't know vedder you like ze job or no. Zo I zink maby you like to gome mit me to spend ze veekend by mine home in Glengoe

[Glenco, Illinois] und look her over before you mage up your mind. I minezelf zink she's looging bretty good, but you might be zinking udderwise." (The last was said with a little self-deprecating smile.)

I was utterly astonished and overwhelmed by the sudden decision of fate to smile on me in my economically precarious situation. A confirmed disbeliever in divine intervention in human affairs, I could not help thinking that, had I not been, I would have been unable to think of anything in either my behavior or my character that could have justified such salvation. Besides, I was genuinely puzzled that anyone would want so earnestly to have an unknown artist paint a picture of his wife, on what I thought was the questionable evidence of competence revealed in that painting of my father. Of course I could not confide these thoughts to Mr. Teich—I could only stammer my thanks for his appreciation of my work, and for his kind invitation. So it was arranged that he and his chauffeur would pick me up on Friday on their way from his plant on the south side to the north shore village, some forty miles from Chicago, where I was to spend the weekend "looging over" Madame Teich.

Of course I took "ze job." She was a very handsome and per-sonable woman, decidedly paintable; and although I could not con-sider myself a portrait painter, I approached this commission with some anticipation of success. She was large, a good many pounds overweight, but with a figure that was definitely voluptuous. In the painting she was to be seated—it would be a three-quarter-length pose. I was sure I would enjoy doing it. Besides, I genuinely liked the subject, her husband, and their two children, a boy and a girl, both young teenagers. They were all interested in the progress of the portrait but agreed not to ask to see it until I should consider it finished. It was always a pleasure to spend the time that the sittings required with this gracious family in their home on the shore of the lake. It became routine that I would be picked up on Fridays and on other appointed days travel out by myself on the Skokie Valley Electric Train. The sittings, which usually lasted about two hours each, sometimes mornings, sometimes afternoons, took place in an upstairs sitting room in the Teich mansion where there was good north light from a large window.

One of the most attractive features of this unusual commission was an unstated emolument in the arrangement that kept me relatively well fed. In the course of the sittings it developed that I would normally share the Teich table on weekends and, more often than not, during the weekday sittings as well. In addition to this bountiful hospitality, I was usually offered a return-trip ticket for the train to Chicago. This thoughtfulness was characteristic of the Teichs and an indication that they fully realized my financial condition. Furthermore, to make it appear that this was not really charity, they would explain that the tickets were quite cheap when bought by the book.

Such liberality made me sometimes wonder if this concern for my welfare might have influenced the commission of the portrait as well; that is, if someone in the background might have sponsored the idea on my behalf, knowing that I needed the work. Of course this was a pretty far-fetched idea. There seemed to be no connection with anyone my family knew and the friend of Mr. Teich's who had introduced my father as a portrait painter simply by his reputation because his friend was looking for an artist to paint his wife's portrait. Then it occurred to me that I had possibly thwarted a commission that might have been intended for my dad. But this idea also seemed to belong in the realm of fantasy. And I knew that he would have renounced any interest in such a commission if he thought he could influence Teich to give me the job. If any of my imaginings did happen to be true, of course, my father would never have let me know it.

As pleasant and fortuitous as the conditions connected with the portrait were, there were some disruptions and setbacks too. The most memorable occurred one morning in December when I reported to the house to keep an appointment for a sitting at ten. I had walked the half mile from the train station in four inches of snow with leaky shoes. The maid who answered the doorbell was startled to see me.

"Why, Mr. Long!" she said. "Didn't Mrs. Teich reach you this morning? I know she was calling you early this morning to tell you she had been called into Chicago for an important meeting and would not be able to pose today." Evidently she hadn't got the message to my landlady before I left, or that sometimes-unreliable woman had failed to relay it to me.

Although most inconvenient, the situation would not have been too serious except for the fact that I had just one nickel—just *one* nickel—in my pocket. I had been counting on the return ticket that was usually provided. There was nothing to do now but walk the few miles, about twelve I believe, to Evanston where the Chicago Elevated system reached its northern terminus. However the fare on that conveyance was *ten* cents. I had never panhandled in my life, but perhaps this was the time to start. I thought deeply about this on that long, dreary, and most uncomfortable trip on freezing feet. The more I thought the less attractive became the idea of asking a stranger for even just a nickel. Then I suddenly remembered that I had an acquaintance in Evanston—a youngish lady I had met on my voyage to France. Through correspondence we had kept in touch, and on my return to the States we had met a few times in Chicago. I had not seen her lately, but I felt sure she would welcome a call from me. I could tell her a plausible story about losing my wallet, and this would solve my dilemma. I would not have to humiliate my ego; after all an innocent little lie would be better than asking a stranger for help.

In Evanston I found a phone booth, deposited my nickel, and dialed the number. The phone at the other end rang: it rang, and rang, and rang, interminably it seemed. Obviously, there was no one home. Exasperated by this added turn of bad luck, I slammed down the receiver with considerable force. There was an instantaneous rain of coins in the return box. I was stupefied with wonder by this sudden change of heart from the gods, whoever they might be. I collected all of eighty-five cents in coins—a veritable bonanza in my situation. I immediately sought warmth, hot food, and drink before boarding the "El" for home. (This was in 1930, when the dollar was worth at least five times what it is today.)

Mrs. Teich was most solicitous and apologetic about what had happened to cause my fruitless trip, but of course she never knew the extent of the consequences. However, there were some other, more serious circumstances that interfered with and delayed my finishing work on the portrait. First, Mrs. Teich fell ill with a flu virus and was unable to pose for several weeks. Unfortunately, time was not the only thing lost. Mrs. Teich shed more than a few pounds during her illness, and this wrought a substantial change in her appearance from that shown in the painting, which had been nearing completion. When we discussed this she confessed that she was greatly pleased by her loss of poundage. She said she was determined to never regain what she had lost, and she fervently hoped I could alter the portrait to correspond to her improved image. This, of course, was not an easy task. It required several more sittings and a great deal of sweat on my part. However, before I could call the picture finished to my satisfaction, there came another hitch.

The Teichs had planned a vacation trip in Europe. They left in early June and were away for five weeks. When they returned, to my dismay, and I suppose to hers, Mrs. Teich, in spite of her resistance, had regained her previous girth. I had to build her up again to her original dimensions. What an inspiration-killing seesaw this had become! If I should ever develop any inclination to become a professional portrait painter, which seems doubtful at best, recollection of this episode would surely dispel it.

But the day finally arrived when "ze job" was finished and presented for approval. I was happy that the reaction of the whole family was very favorable, but I couldn't resist wondering if they might not be just as relieved as I was that the long, drawn-out project was ended at last. The portrait was ultimately surrounded with an elaborately carved gold frame, which I could not consider very appropriate; but it was obviously very expensive, and I consoled myself that it served to demonstrate what the patron thought of the painting's worth.

When I was asked to present a bill for my efforts I was at sea. On one hand there were the seemingly endless delays that had prolonged the work interminably, not to mention the discomforts I suffered; on the other were the numerous kindnesses and courtesies to consider: the train tickets and the intermittent hospitality of bed and board over that long period. A businesslike calculation was impossible from my standpoint. I let Mr. Teich know that I would have to leave this detail entirely in his hands, and that I would be satisfied with any sum he might consider fair. He mailed his check for $500—a very handsome and generous settlement I thought. To me, this represented a small fortune, and it actually was, considering the value of the dollar during that period. Although I was sure the Teichs were well satisfied with the portrait, I was not too happy with it. I considered it a good likeness and interpretation of character, but I felt that in its having been reworked drastically twice, it had lost the freshness and spontaneity that my enthusiasm had begun to express initially. Still, the experience had been both enjoyable and enlightening. It also had allowed me to exist as an artist, whereas without it I might well have failed to pursue what I considered my destiny.

But $500, bounteous as it seemed, lasted a discouragingly short time. I had forgotten about some bills I owed and the dilapidated state of my very limited wardrobe. Most of the latter was threadbare and definitely required replacement. In addition, my supply of colors, canvas, and other necessary materials had to be replenished if I was to produce the works I had in my head. It was autumn and I began to be depressed again about prospects for my survival as an artist during the coming winter. At this moment and many others like it I was assailed with doubt about the future—not just my own, but that of my friends in the arts as well. Such moments would always lead to a bitter philosophical discontent with the status of the arts, as affected by the economy and the political situation. There was nothing unusual in this. Other artists, and in fact the whole of society, were beginning to sorely doubt what the future might have in store for America as a whole. The term *depression* applied not only to the economy—it applied as well to the mental state of the nation as a whole.

CHAPTER 2
I Receive My First
Mural Commission

I WAS IN JUST SUCH A MENTAL STATE when I was invited to one of the ever-recurring parties in the neighborhood. These parties were sponsored by first one, then another of the few who had quarters that could accommodate several invited people at once. Everyone brought refreshments and shared with everyone else. The feeling of camaraderie was engendered by the fact that everyone was in the same boat. Only occasionally was there anything to celebrate. This one celebrated the momentary success of a writer I knew. He had found a job as a proofreader in a small publishing house.

It was during that somewhat alcoholic evening that I became acquainted with Ray Burns—a young fellow who worked in the firm of the well-known architect Phillip B. Maher. He had not had the job long but seemed to be making a success of it. For some reason, he seemed interested in the fact that I was a painter. As the party broke up, he said he would like very much to see some of my work; so we went together to my nearby studio. I imagined that it was his stimulated condition that prompted his effusive admiration of the paintings I showed him, although at the time I had to believe, of course, that he did discuss them very intelligently.

Several days later I was genuinely surprised when he showed up at my door and suggested we go to lunch together. During the meal he confided that his employer was just completing a mansion on the lakeshore for the mayor of Wilmette, a north shore village near Chicago. The plans called for murals to be painted in a large recreation room on the ground floor. He wanted Ray, his office manager, to contact qualified artists who might be interested in the project, and Ray said he had immediately thought of me. He said that he would have to contact and interview other artists, but he hoped I might be interested since he liked my work so much. Once all the entries were in hand, the architect would then review them and select the most appropriate and professional design. I said that certainly I was interested and appreciative of the opportunity. I did not reveal my congenital lack of enthusiasm for the mural medium and my lack of experience in that field.

Ray volunteered to drive me out to Wilmette the next day to view the spaces for the murals in the palatial residence that was nearing completion. On the way, I learned the mayor's unbelievable name was Carbon Petroleum Dubbs (no kidding). To account for this was the fact that his father had been a petroleum engineer when his talented son, the mayor, was born. The son had carried on the dream of his father and had perfected the Dubbs "cracking" process, now being used universally in extracting and refining gasoline from crude oil. This had recently brought Carbon Petroleum the fortune that made his palatial residence possible. Carbon Petroleum shared his father's pride in his profession, for there was now a teenage Carbon Petroleum, Jr., heir to the Dubbs family fortune.

The house was vast. It had three floors, an elevator, and a switch-board with forty telephone extensions. There was a map room with a three-foot-diameter revolving globe, a card room, and an indoor swimming pool, for use when the weather would not permit swim-ming in the lake or basking in the sun on the beach below the house. And these were only the most impressive of the mansion's numerous manifestations of wealth and luxury.

The architectural structure of the house was finished, but there were workmen everywhere: hanging doors; installing windows; com-pleting the wiring system, the air conditioning, the plumbing— everything in fact to make the living space not only conveniently habitable but luxuriously comfortable both inside and out. There was work going on in the recreation room too; but from the interior decorator's designs, which Ray had brought along, the room when finished could be clearly visualized. It was a full hundred feet square, with a tomato red carpet nine feet wide running completely around a terrazzo dance floor laid in cream-colored squares, with a large points-of-the-compass design in the center. The east wall facing the lake was composed almost entirely of plate glass, with wide French doors at each end opening on the terrace. On the south wall a cavernous fireplace, faced in black granite, was centered. The north wall had a huge mirror installed in its center. The decorator's sketches, executed in color, showed a sofa, covered with dark blue and white vertically striped material, situated at the base of the mirror and running its entire twenty-foot length. The stripes in the upholstery were a foot wide. The sofa against the north wall was balanced by one covered with red and white vertically striped material in front of the fireplace.

It was the spaces surrounding the mirror on the north wall and the fireplace on the south wall that were to be decorated with murals. These were going to be rather awkward spaces to fill, especially the ones surrounding the mirror, where a long narrow space at the top connected with two fairly large panels on each side. I was furnished with blueprint elevations of the two walls that gave the exact measurements of the mural spaces, and almost immediately on returning to my studio I began working on the preliminary sketches of the subject matter to be fitted into these dimensions.

After a few false starts I came up with the idea of a circus scene for the larger space around the mirror and a jungle scene for the smaller one. These ideas were fully developed in sketches drawn to a scale of one foot to one inch. The red, white, and blue color scheme of the room dictated the use of brilliant color in the murals. The two panels were closely related by the subject matter. Both featured wild animals and humans, combined in comical situations to create a spirit of humor and gaiety in harmony with the purpose of the room.

The larger mural illustrated a three-ring circus going on in the large spaces on each side of the mirror. These were connected by two trapeze performers swinging to join hands in the long narrow space at the top, helping to create the illusion of a single scene, with the center cut off from view by the mirror. Comedy was expressed in the circus mural by the antics of the clowns, the fat lady, and other freaks. In one incident, a pickpocket plies his trade on an unaware victim.

The jungle scene on the opposite side of the room was much easier to compose. It was interrupted only by the fireplace in the lower center, and the two small spaces on each side extending to the floor were easily fitted into the design. Here there were hunters facing impossible odds: being charged by a rhinoceros from behind while aiming at a snarling tiger in front, and being chased by a lion over a cliff while suffering a pelting with coconuts from a monkey in a palm tree.

I was pleased with the total effect of the two murals, which I felt was in perfect harmony with the kinds of social events that could be expected to take place in the room. I wondered too if any of the other competing artists might choose similar subjects.

When the sketches were finished I delivered them to Ray at the architect's office, which was only a short distance from my studio. I watched his expression while he looked at them. Finally he smiled and said he thought I had handled the problem very well indeed. He went on to say there were three other artists to be heard from, but that he had set a deadline for them of Friday (it was then Tuesday). He said the Dubbses were very anxious to have the house finished and wouldn't dally over a decision about the murals, and he would let me know Dubbs's response to the sketches the following Monday.

To me it seemed a long and anxious wait. I could not get my mind on much else. I resented this project's preventing my progress on a painting I had under way, but I simply was too much aware of what failure to win this commission would mean. At this point it was vital. But when Ray finally called on Monday and asked me to come to his office, I could not help feeling that my sketches must have won, and this was in fact the case. When he gave me the news he seemed almost as pleased as I was. He said the Dubbses had let themselves show some enthusiasm for my designs. They liked the subject matter in particular as being just right for the gay spirit of the room.

Nothing was said about my fee for the murals, and I hesitated to bring it up, thinking it would be discussed at what was considered the proper time. It was a little later that it came out that Maher had given Dubbs an overall figure for the decorating part of his contract and that the amount to be expended for the murals was set at $800. This was perfectly satisfactory to me, but I felt I should have at least been asked if it were. Oh well, I was in no position to show my feeling of having been slighted. I was just happy that I was to be paid what I considered a fairly handsome sum, although it would be considered a pittance today for such a commission.

So I was back again to riding the north shore electric train, this time to Wilmette, the first village north of Evanston by a few of the miles I had walked in the snow the winter before. It was still a long walk from the station to the site of my mural job, but it was nice fall weather and the walk was exercise that I enjoyed. However, I could not look forward with pleasure to contact with the Dubbses as I had with the Teichs. I seldom saw anyone but Dubbs himself; he came in the recreation room fairly often to watch me work but never spoke to me nor had any comment. I had been told by Ray that Dubbs, who thought he knew a great deal about building construction, and probably did, believed he could save a good deal of money by letting the contract on what is called a "cost plus" basis. In this arrangement the contractor agrees to do the work for the actual cost of materials and labor, plus an overall fee for services and expertise. Dubbs thought he could save by buying the materials himself and inspecting the work as it progressed to see that it was done properly and expeditiously.

It developed that he was badly mistaken. During the depression, everyone who had a job, a contract, or a business was trying every expedient to make it last just as long as possible. It became obvious to me that this prevailing attitude was slowing down progress on the Dubbs mansion. For example, before the large sheets of plate glass that formed the east wall of the recreation room were crisscrossed with the usual white stripes to make them visible, a workman with a heavy ladder demolished one when he tried to walk through what he said he thought was a vacant space. Of more concern to me were repairs to areas adjacent to the murals, as these interrupted my work. At one point an improperly installed drain on the terrace above the rec room leaked through the ceiling, a large area of which had to be torn out and replaced. This was very near one of the murals, and I had to lose two days while the damage was repaired. Not only that, but it was no sooner fixed than it leaked again after a heavy rain and the repairs had to be duplicated. There were several other similar mistakes or mishaps in other parts of the building, too many to have all been accidental it seemed. Dubbs swore and tore his hair. He knew he was being had, but there was not a thing he could do about it.

My work on the mural went very well except for these holdups. I painted directly on the wall with hand-ground colors thinned with turpentine to give a matte finish. The surface of the wall was ideal. The walls and ceiling of the room had been covered with thin canvas before being painted with several thin coats. This produced a very smooth surface for me to work on, of the sort that does not allow cracks to develop. The pigments I used would be quite permanent when protected with a coat of matte picture varnish.

My contract called for the painting contractor to furnish all required scaffolding for my work as well as protective covering under my work areas to shield the floor from accidental drips and spills of my materials. The painting contractor was very cooperative. He had covered not only my work areas but the whole floor with heavy two-ply waterproof construction paper.

One day there was an unforeseen and somewhat disturbing development. As I was working near the top of one of the panels, a rather stern-faced man appeared below. He reached up and handed me his card, which identified him as a union official. He asked if I were a member of the local painters and decorators union. I admitted I was not. He hinted strongly that I had better become one. It had never occurred to me that I would encounter this requirement on a private residential job, but it seemed that this was such an extensive project that nearly all the trade unions had become involved. The fact that I was an individual "fine" artist, who normally worked in my own studio, seemed to cut no ice at all. I was worried because I knew there were large initiation and membership fees involved in joining a union that I could not afford, to say nothing of the monthly dues. The next day Dubbs asked me about union membership and I made the same admission. He said, rather bleakly, "You really ought to belong, you know. This is a completely unionized job."

In spite of worrying, I was determined not to join the union. I not only knew I could not afford the fees—I also knew the unions in the Chicago area were practically all in the hands of gangsters and racketeers. I rebelled at contributing anything to their interests. But what was I to do? I thought about the long walk from the station to the Dubbs project. It was mainly through a relatively deserted area; a perfect place to get picked up by someone who insisted on my becoming a union member.

Today, I am not proud to confess that I started carrying a forty-five-caliber automatic pistol that I had owned ever since coming to Chicago. At that time, in my juvenile reasoning, it seemed my only recourse in a bad situation. How foolhardy youth can be—and how lucky. Strangely enough, there were no further developments. I could explain this only by reasoning that Dubbs had unexpectedly swung his weight, which was considerable, to have the matter dropped. I thought it very possible that he didn't want any further trouble on his project; he had enough to contend with as it was.

There was a striking contrast between the Dubbses and the Teichs in their attitudes toward the person who was creating a work of art at their bidding. While my relationship with the Teichs had been quite pleasant, it was very different with the Dubbses. In my contacts with members of the family it became very apparent that I was held in an inferior position in their esteem, no more nor less noteworthy than any other workman on the job. They would bring friends in to see the room and the work, but I was never introduced to the visitors or referred to in any way.

At one point, Mrs. Dubbs came to me with a request that I paint a likeness of one of her children on the face of a boy in the circus midway scene. I pointed out that the image would be so small when seen from a distance that the likeness would be totally lost. She then showed me a miniature of her boy, painted on ivory, to prove that such work was certainly possible. She obviously implied that what she wanted was simply beyond my ability. She could not recognize the fact that a miniature likeness has no place as an element of a mural decoration.

It happened one day when Dubbs was watching me work that I accidentally overturned the can in which I kept my brushes standing in turpentine. He asked immediately if the turpentine would harm the floor. I assured him it would not, that it would act as a cleaning agent if anything; I also pointed out that the floor was covered. He seemed unconvinced.

It was on a Saturday in late October that I could call the murals finished to my approximate satisfaction and, I must admit, to my relief. I was always a bit apprehensive about the possibility of trouble with the union. Also, I was not at all sure of the Dubbses' complete approval, in spite of having received no negative static during the course of the work. None of the family was around when I gathered up my materials and equipment and departed. I notified Ray that he could tell his boss I awaited his approval and my check.

Several days later Ray called me. He said they had my check from Dubbs, but that he had withheld a hundred dollars for damage he claimed I had done to the floor. He suggested that we call and let

Dubbs know that we would come out that day to discuss the matter, if it was convenient. (Apparently there was no problem with the murals themselves.) On the way out in his car I told Ray about the incident with the spilled turpentine. I had been thinking, and I was sure I now knew what had caused the trouble; it could not have been the spilled turpentine itself. Sure enough, when we arrived and I examined the material used to protect the floor the cause was apparent.

Dubbs was called and he came in scowling. He pointed to the spot on the floor under the mural and asked if I denied I had caused it. I told him that I disclaimed responsibility for it. He grew red in the face and almost shouted, "Why, I saw you myself carelessly overturn a can of turpentine in that exact spot." Before I could answer he went on, "Mr. Long I have observed all the time you were working here. It is obvious that you think you are better than any of the other workmen on this job. You have shown no regard whatever for their work. I believe the men who laid this floor are just as much artists as you are."

I replied that any discussion of opinions about aesthetics was beside the point, that the problem was simply to decide who was responsible for damage to the floor. I reminded him that my contract called for the painting contractor to furnish adequate protective covering for the floor under the murals. The cover had been pulled aside to reveal the damage. I raised one corner and showed that the paper had a tar center to make it waterproof.

"Furthermore," I said, "if you will look closely at the surface of the rest of the floor you will see that it has been slightly discolored all over by the tar in the center of the paper partially melting during the hot summer weather. You can even see the lines made by the joints in the paper. If you want to be paid for damage to the floor, you will have to look to the painting contractor."

The man was furious. We had become the center of attention of the group of workmen in the room, and he was losing face in this confrontation. He was so disconcerted he could not trust himself to speak. He simply uttered an incoherent sound that resembled a croak, turned, and marched off with long strides that punctuated his anger and frustration. I actually had to feel sorry for this rather pitiful millionaire.

On the way home, Ray told me he knew that the painting contractor was a longtime friend of Dubbs's and that Dubbs would be loath to hold him responsible for the damage. He said he was afraid I would have to sue Dubbs to retrieve the hundred dollars. But he suggested I consult a lawyer. I just happened to be very friendly with a young lawyer who was a brother of a girl I was going with at the time. My luck held. He was able to get a decision in the city small claims court with no trouble, as the evidence was very clear. And he refused to charge anything at all. I must admit, however, that although I was not to blame for the stain, I should have realized the floor covering was not adequate when I examined it the first time. I just didn't realize the turpentine would soak through the upper layer and dissolve the tar center.

Thus ends the story of my first venture into the world of mural painting, although there was an epilogue. Sometime later Ray said Dubbs had asked him to tell me he would like to talk with me. Neither of us could imagine why. Of course I never seriously considered contacting him for an appointment. Curious though I might be, too many of the possibilities were unpleasant to contemplate. Much later I was surprised when the magazine *American Architect* ran a story on the Dubbs mansion. It featured the recreation room, including some fairly good photographs of the murals.

When I reviewed the total episode, I realized it had been worthwhile for more than financial reasons. I had learned a great deal, although I still could not consider mural painting a stimulating field for my talent. I had been intrigued by the problems the project had presented. Solving them, particularly figuring out how to fit appropriate subject matter into the interrupted rectangles of the mural panels, was an exercise in space relationships that would apply to the abstract elements of design in any kind of painting. I was glad to have had the experience, although it had applied principally to mural painting. I realized that in spite of my preferences there might well be other murals in my artistic future.

I remember clearly my mental state at that particular juncture of my career. I knew very well what I wanted to do as an artist. It might be said that I was unambitious. I did not look forward to great fame or fortune; in my philosophy the only permissible ambition for an artist is to develop his talent to the greatest possible degree. I did not have the illusion that I was a great artist or had the ability to become one. I only knew that I wanted to make every possible effort to continue painting. I could see that under the prevailing economic conditions there was very little for a beginning artist to be encouraged about as far as a career was concerned. I knew the direction I wanted to follow but realized that if I achieved my objective I could hardly expect my kind of painting to support me. Some painters that I knew with similar ambitions had resorted to a search for work in some form of commercial art in spite of the economy, and in spite of their reservations that this was a degradation of their talent. Some were successful, but I knew they were basically unhappy. I had no inclination to follow this course. But I did realize I would have to find at least temporary work in some other field. However, jobs were scarce in any field, and only those with some experience had any chance of being hired for the few that were vacant.

I still seemed to be lucky. A friend steered me to a part-time job he was leaving to return to his family home where he had a better job offer. I worked as a sort of head waiter in Harding's Men's Grill on Wabash Avenue in the heart of "the loop" from four to eight each evening. My responsibility was to seat the patrons, being sure they were equally distributed to the five waiters' tables, and to write all the meal checks. I also had to set up all the displays in the refrigerated showcase at the entrance to the downstairs grill. These consisted of fresh cuts of meat, such as steaks and roasts, and the fresh raw fruits and vegetables that accompanied them when they were all "deliciously prepared" and served together as choices from the menu. My artistic talent bore fruit here, so to speak, and I was congratulated by my employer for the "artistry" of my compositions. I received the munificent reward of two meals a day from the grill and eight dollars a week.

I kept this job for several months. It enabled me to stretch the money from the Dubbs mural through the winter and to continue painting almost every day. I felt I was making progress. Then in the spring, I had word from my father that he had taken a contract to decorate a new movie theater in Lexington, Kentucky, and that he could offer me a job helping with it. This was a very attractive offer, and of course I was very happy. I was still quite young, and immature in some respects. I was sometimes more than a little homesick at being away from home for long periods. Returning to Kentucky would satisfy my longing for the paternal roof, and I knew how much it would gratify my mother and father. There was only one drawback; I knew that I would have very little opportunity to devote time to my own work as a painter. But this would no doubt continue to be my fate as long as it should remain necessary to make a living by some other means.

CHAPTER 3

I Continue Painting and
Discover Berea

I WAS ABLE TO FIND SOMEONE to replace me at the Grill; I give up the studio that I had been occupying alone for the past few months; and in a very short time I was reunited with my parents. It was a happy reunion. My mother and father had missed me even more than I had missed them, I suspect. They were both well—she in her sixties, he ten years older. They had come to Kentucky a few years before from Knoxville, Tennessee, where they had lived off and on for a good many years before I was born there. They had made the move to Kentucky when my father became acquainted with some of the area's horse owners and began to receive commissions to paint both the owners and their famous horses.

He had had a colorful and varied career as both an artist and a sportsman, and he loved the outdoor life. He had bred and raised champion bird dogs and was an expert with both rod and gun. He often said he was an artist because it fitted his way of life and supported his love of hunting and fishing. He admitted that the latter amounted to an obsession that overshadowed his desire to paint. But he had done many kinds of painting, in addition to portraits. His landscapes, reminiscent of those of Corot and Turner, were among his best works. His talent was such that he could adapt it to any artistic or economic situation. When times were tough he had no difficulty finding employment with outdoor advertising companies as a pictorial sign painter. In those days, before full-color lithography on a large scale, all scenic "bulletin boards" were necessarily painted by hand.

He also occasionally designed and painted the many sets of scenery used by the drama theaters of earlier days. These were in the form of decorated curtains, raised and lowered to present appropriate backgrounds for various scenes of the plays that were performed. He also would often decorate or redecorate the whole interior of a theater.

The contract for which he planned to use my help was of this latter type. A local movie theater was to be redecorated, and my father's design included some small vignette murals on the side walls of the interior. These vignettes consisted of little more than simple scenes reflecting the theatrical atmosphere. At this point I do not have a clear recollection of their final effect, but I remember that the management of the theater and my father were well pleased with the job I did.

At one point, when I was on the scaffold working on the wall, a young man called to me from below. He asked if he could talk to me about taking painting lessons; he said he had spoken to my father, who had referred him to me. I descended from the scaffold, and we discussed the matter at length while occupying theater seats.

He introduced himself as Bert Mullins from Berea, a college town forty miles south of Lexington. Bert was rather striking in appearance—fairly tall, with straight black hair, black eyes, and dark skin. I learned later that there was some Indian blood in his ancestry. What struck me most about him was his intensity when he spoke, in spite of an impression of overall shyness. He explained that he had heard of my father, and since he had all his life wanted to paint, he thought this might be an opportunity to study with a professional artist. My father had explained that he did not do any teaching, but he suggested that I, his son, might be willing to give lessons and, of course, recommended me highly. I judged the man to be in his late twenties—a few years older than I. His speech immediately identified him as a Kentucky mountaineer, and his manner was what I would describe as almost charming. At the end of the interview, which I found most interesting, it was arranged that Bert would come to Lexington for his first lesson the following Sunday. He was employed by Berea College, famous among other things for its woodworking department where reproductions of early American furniture were created. Because of his job as a master turner, Bert would be able to come for lessons only on Sundays, but he hoped to be able to do so for an indefinitely extended period. I could promise only that I would be available for as long as I should remain in Lexington, since I could not be sure when I might leave.

To the first lesson Bert brought some sketches, a few fully developed drawings, and two or three paintings in oil. His interest was centered on portraiture. I believe he had attended the Berea College Academy for two years. The academy was the equivalent of most high schools, but there was very little time devoted to art on that level. So we started with the basics: color theory, perspective, composition. Of course not a lot of progress can be made in one afternoon a week; but I could see at once that in spite of his ignorance in these areas, Bert had a real natural talent that would hasten his progress. Above all, he had a burning desire to improve and develop his abilities as far as possible. I could not claim to be a professionally trained teacher, but I was sure I could help a great deal in the process.

We soon developed a warm friendship in our student-teacher relationship. Although Bert had had little formal education, he had done a lot of reading. He was, rather surprisingly, interested in poetry and literature, particularly that of the nineteenth-century writers. He was interested as well in the painters of the same period—the romanticists. We often engaged in long discussions, which seemed to strengthen our relationship, although our critical views were necessarily quite different. Our growing friendship resulted in Bert's inviting me to spend a weekend in Berea with him and his wife. The visit offered me a pleasant introduction not only to Eva, but also to the town, which I had not seen before.

Before my father had finished work on the theater, a small coincidence occurred. One day on a Lexington street, I saw a man I was sure I recognized from the past. I had not known him well, but he proved to have been an administrator at the Chicago Art Institute when I was a student there. I stopped him and introduced myself. He was Henry Warder Rannells; I recalled his name very well, but I was surprised when he remembered mine and seemed pleased to know that I was pursuing my art career in that area. He explained that he was the new head of the art department at the University of Kentucky, in Lexington, and had been there only a short time. He ended the conversation by asking me to keep in touch and to give him my phone number.

This turned out to be a very fortunate meeting for me. Later, just as I was planning to return to Chicago, I received a call from him asking me to come to his office at the university to discuss something in which he thought I might be interested. Of course I was consumed by curiosity, wondering what the something could possibly be.

At the start of the interview, Rannells said he remembered some drawings I had made in one of the life classes. These had been displayed in the student show at the end of my second year at the Institute. I was amazed, not only at what seemed an unusual feat of recall, but also that he had thought the drawings worth remembering. He went on to explain that the government had recently set up a program designed to give professional artists employment during the depression. Under this program, called Public Works of Art Projects, or PWAP, various institutions such as universities, libraries, and city or state governments were extended grants for the decoration of new buildings. The University of Kentucky had been given such a grant to be used in the creation of murals in two of its recently completed buildings.

One of the places selected by the university to be decorated was the Browsing Room of the new Margaret I. King Library. Rannells explained that he, as head of the art department, had been put in charge of this program at the university. He said that the government, contrary to its usual procedure on other types of grants, attached no strings to these grants and that the university had been given a free hand in selecting the artists to do the work. The artists would be paid by the government what was considered to be a living wage at that time, and they would be paid for as long as the individual projects might require for completion.

Rannells admitted that he knew nothing about my work after I had left the Institute, but he somehow had confidence that if I was interested I could create designs for the two murals he had in mind for the Browsing Room that would be approved by the art department and the president of the university. He wondered, diplomatically, if the proposal might interest me—that is, if I was in a position to accept it if it did? After I had assured him that I was indeed interested, he asked if I had had any experience in mural painting. In answer, I told him about the Dubbs mural and the very modest project in the local theater that I was just then finishing. I also mentioned the article in *American Architect*, with photos of the Dubbs murals. He expressed great interest in seeing these, and I promised to bring them to our next meeting. He also said he would visit the theater, though I explained that my work there was hardly a good example of my skill as a muralist. He smiled and said he realized that.

From his office we went to the library to look at the mural spaces, which proved to be above bookshelves set into the wall at each end of a hundred-foot-long, comparatively narrow room. Each of the bookcases was topped by a Georgian broken pediment (the style of the architecture was Early American Georgian) that extended into the mural space. Such pediments usually contain pedestals, on each of which is placed a sculptured bust of some personage. Rannells said this could be expected here, and that I would have to devise some way of dealing with the busts in my designs. Since the room would be in almost constant use, doing the murals in place would be impossible; the necessary scaffolding would prevent access to the books on the shelves below. The murals would have to be painted on canvas elsewhere, then mounted in place.

Our work in the theater was finished shortly afterward, and I immediately turned my attention to the sketches for the murals. I was put on the government payroll at that point, even though the sketches would have to be approved before I could start work on the murals. I do not remember how long it took to finish the sketches, nor what the wage was, but I had to do some research before I could select a subject. I finally decided on "Rural Life in Eastern Kentucky"—that is to say, the Cumberland Mountain region where many students of the university had come from. I wanted to show the life of this area, where the customs and culture of the original settlers had been preserved to a remarkable degree. I discussed this selection with Rannells and was gratified that he felt it was highly appropriate.

I believe the sketches required two or three weeks to finish to my satisfaction. But there was a hitch in proceeding with the murals. Dr. Frank McVey, the president of the university, would not approve one of the designs. It included some elements that referred to the continuing existence of the traditional, violent family feuds of the region. He feared the negative reaction of a large proportion of the public if the design were used. When I gave this serious consideration, I had to believe that he was justified in his conclusion, and I agreed to make a new design, which the president ultimately approved. In the final designs, one scene represented "Labor" and the other "Recreation." The new version required a week to finish.

I then had to find a workroom where I could do the painting. Since the panels were ten and a half feet tall, few rooms were of sufficient

"Labor" panel, University of Kentucky Library, Louisville.
Photograph by M. S. Rezny.

"Recreation" panel, University of Kentucky Library, Louisville.
Photograph by M. S. Rezny.

height, and none were available, apparently, in town. This began to look like an insurmountable difficulty. Strangely, my search for a workroom set the stage for a move that was to affect the course of my life profoundly.

It was Bert Mullins (he continued to come to Lexington for his Sunday lessons) who found an answer to the dilemma. He knew of a vacant space over the Berea Bank and Trust Company that he was sure had very high ceilings. He eagerly suggested that I come to Berea with him to examine the space when his lesson was finished that day, and I accepted the invitation. Eva further invited me to stay with them until the studio question was settled.

When I measured the height of the ceiling the next day, I groaned. It was exactly ten feet; the panels were six inches taller. But wait! There was a skylight, and its well extended up two more feet. It was wide enough for a panel's semicircular top to fit into it with a little room to spare on the sides. The day was saved!

The space contained two rooms—a normal-size entry room and a very large studio room, both with large skylights. It also contained a storeroom and a washroom with running water. The toilet facility, available to the occupants of this upper story and to the public as well, was directly across the hall. There had been two large windows in the outer wall of the large room, but these had been closed off by a recently added second story to the building next door. This was why the space was now vacant. It had been occupied by the Ogg Photographic Studio, but the photographer said he needed the side light from those windows for his work, so he moved when they were sealed off. I saw at once that the layout would be ideal for my requirements.

Bert was joyous over the fact that my moving to Berea would offer an opportunity for him to study with me under much more favorable conditions and for a longer period. He would also be able to learn a great deal by watching, and perhaps even assisting in, the painting of the murals. I believe, too, that he looked forward to a closer association with me as his friend and mentor. Although he was a few years older than me, neither of us was conscious of this difference. I was also pleased with the opportunity to get to know Bert better and to try to help him develop his talent—which he wanted so much to do. I was not long in discovering him to be a unique and fascinating personality.

I also soon realized that he had gained quite a reputation locally as an artist. He had not told me about the several paintings on which his fame was based. One was a small mural in the local Baptist church that served as a background for the baptismal font. These scenic backgrounds, incidentally, were to be seen in Baptist churches throughout the South. Many were painted by local amateur artists, or by itinerant sign painters who made this a part of their business. In Bert's case, the mural in the church and a copy he had made of a well-known painting of Christ in the garden were his principal works. Through these, several portraits of friends, and a few landscapes, he was considered by the community to be as much an artist as the fine craftsman that he most certainly was. He could do anything in the art of woodworking with great skill and artistry. He had created many fine pieces of furniture for himself and Eva and for others in the area. As master turner in the woodworking department of Berea College, famous for its reproductions of early American furniture, he was responsible for all the turning of table legs, bedposts, and similar features, so it could be said that his work enjoyed universal, though largely anonymous, recognition. But even if he had been celebrated for these accomplishments, this would not have satisfied Bert. He had a burning desire to express his creative urge in what he knew was called "fine art." I believe he had a still greater desire to become well known as a fine artist, not just a fine craftsman.

I soon came to the rather disturbing conclusion that Bert would rather not reveal that he was my pupil. He introduced me as an artist friend he had met in Lexington. It appeared that he had never mentioned his weekly lessons to his friends, and it dawned on me that he was expecting me to understand and go along with this deception. At first I was very much surprised—then I was amused by it. Finally, I was able to understand it, as I began to understand Bert's very complex personality. And I also began to feel that it could actually strengthen our friendship to share in this little deception in which we were thought of as colleagues rather than as teacher and pupil. If it helped Bert's self-image that much, I was willing to go along with it.

The move from Lexington to the studio over the bank was accomplished without delay or difficulty. There were regrets on both sides over leaving my parents, but I assured them they could expect me to visit them frequently as long as I should remain in Berea. They were elated over what they saw as a successful beginning of my career as an artist. My father's pride was inordinate. It was his conviction that I had inherited my talent from him, that I was destined to become a world-renowned artist, and that he would be able to bask in my glory. What a happy delusion!

My first and most important concern in Berea was to become acquainted with the town and its inhabitants. Bert made every effort to see that this introduction was pleasant and successful. But it was an ongoing process that, in the end, required weeks and months rather than days. He began by introducing me to his best friends and foremost acquaintances among college personnel and other inhabitants of the town. I believe that at that time the population was about fourteen hundred.

The town of Berea and Berea College had been founded as the result of one man's almost unbelievable courage in remaining true to his ideals in the face of threats on his life. John G. Fee, Jr., was an abolitionist preacher who first succeeded in preaching the gospel on land he owned, which included the present site of the college and the town. The college was founded in the 1850s, at a time when the entire country was facing the slavery problem, and the story of its founding and of the community is well known in the annals of Kentucky history. Black students were accepted in the college from its start and until 1904, when the Kentucky Day Law excluded them. It was not until 1963 that the Day Law was rescinded and black students again appeared on the campus. The school is and has always been a basically religious institution, but nondenominational.

The college is known far and wide as a model for the practice of the work ethic in modern education. It was founded with the avowed purpose of giving impoverished young people of the Appalachian Mountains region an opportunity to gain an education by allowing them to pay all their costs through their labor. The program provides a number of "Student Industries" for this purpose. These have included baking, candy making, woodworking, broom making, metalworking, and weaving, as well as the operation of a laundry, a newspaper, a hotel, a maintenance plant, and the town fire department, among other operations. In addition to being able to pay for their general and higher education by working in these industries and occupations, students can learn a useful skill in an occupation they might wish to follow after graduation. At the same time, the labor they provide and the income from the various industries go a long way toward covering the costs of operating the college.

I was greatly impressed by this program and the ability and sincerity of those who managed it. I must admit, however, that having been unable to subscribe to fundamental biblical beliefs almost from birth, I had reservations about the heavy emphasis placed on this element in the college. Fortunately, I was smart enough to refrain from expressing my doubts in this religious environment.

The population of the town, including the college, was composed almost entirely of descendants of early settlers of the region. Because of my familiarity with people of the same stock in my native Tennessee mountains, I did not have the problem most strangers have who may wish to be accepted by the community. Of course, I am speaking of a period more than fifty years ago, and the atmosphere in Berea today may be significantly altered. But the indigenous population of eastern Kentucky is fundamentally very conservative, tending to be suspicious of anything new or different. I was fortunate that through my previous contact with Appalachian Mountain people I knew something of their historical background and much about their folklore, music, handicrafts, customs, and vernacular language. I could converse easily, using terms and expressions people were familiar with. I did not of course imitate their accents or ungrammatical language, but apparently they deduced that I must have come from a background similar to their own. I am sure this helped a great deal in my apparently easy acceptance by the kind of community that is normally slow to welcome newcomers to equal social status.

This factor in my favor also seemed to overcome the tendency of most conservative people to look askance at the unknown and unusual. It is certain that I, as a professional artist, would normally have been placed in that category. But this tendency was also offset by the recent establishment of an excellent art department in the college. It was housed in a new, modern building with an art gallery and excellent facilities for teaching. Through this influence the town had become much more conscious of the arts and of artistic values than it had been previously. Because of this, perhaps it did not seem quite so strange to rub elbows with a real, live, professional artist.

Naturally, the art department made the town much more attractive to me than it would have been without it. Among my first friends were Mary Ela, the department head, and her staff of three teachers. They all seemed enthusiastic over the fact that I had decided to paint the murals for the University of Kentucky in Berea. They seemed to hope, as I did, that a close relationship would develop between us, and Mary Ela offered to assist in any practical way possible with the production of the murals.

Bert also saw to it that I met the personnel of the woodworking department and of the other craft departments and student industries. Later on I was to become acquainted with most of the professors, and in due time I met William J. Hutchins himself, the president of the college.

The process of becoming oriented included the whole area—not just the town and its people but the natural features and environment as well. Bert and I went on long exploratory hikes over the surrounding terrain—the first upward thrust of the Cumberland Mountain foothills. By car we visited some of the outlying communities, among them Bert's family home near Disputanta, not far from Berea on Clear Creek in Rockcastle County. This orientation soon convinced me that I had found a setting that I hoped might become reasonably permanent—if not now, perhaps some day, some time.

I had never been happy in Chicago, or any other big city. I longed persistently for the "great outdoors" in which I had spent much of my early life. Like my father, I was an ardent hunter and fisherman, though with me these pastimes never became the obsession that possessed him. The rugged forested areas near Berea offered many opportunities to indulge these interests, as well as endless vistas of natural beauty and deep wooded valleys, corridors of rugged, rocky architecture to delight the eye of any artist. Added to this, I found the people I had met both agreeable and interesting. I knew that future relations with them had every likelihood of being pleasant and stimulating. However, being obliged to go to work immediately on the university murals left me little time to investigate all the possibilities of this new environment.

At this point I was hoping that something would happen to make it possible for me to continue indefinitely in Berea after this job was finished. However, I was keenly aware that if no new commission should suddenly develop I would have to find some other kind of work simply to survive. I had to face the fact that Chicago would offer far better opportunities in this respect than Kentucky, and that I would probably be forced to return there permanently to find a job.

The first thing I needed to do to begin work on the murals was to obtain the necessary materials. I had to have the stretcher frames made for the canvases and to purchase the canvas to cover them. For the latter I made a trip to Lexington, where I was able to obtain cotton canvas duck. Because the material was available in maximum widths of only five feet, two strips had to be sewn together to gain the required width. This created a seam running through the vertical center of the panels. After the canvas was stretched on the frames, the seams were filled with the zinc white oil ground material before the panels were given their final coating over the glue size undercoat. Thus the seams were made invisible to the eye in the final painting.

I had to send to Chicago for several items of my equipment and my hand-ground oil colors and painting mediums. A good friend of mine had volunteered to keep these for me when I left there for Kentucky. We never dreamed I would need them before I returned, but my friend was more than willing to assist by sending them.

Bert was especially interested in the fact that I had manufactured the oil colors myself. While studying in France I had visited the shops where hand grinding of artists' oil colors was carried out. I was fascinated as I watched thick color paste being ground to the proper consistency. First a small electric machine mixed a dry pigment with linseed oil to produce the thick paste. Next, a workman would deposit small dabs of this mixture over most of the surface of a granite slab some three feet square by about four inches thick. He then used what is called a muller (*molette* in French) to grind the color. The muller is shaped like an apothecary's pestle, which fits into a mortar to grind and mix medications. But the bottom of the muller is perfectly flat, rather than rounded like that of the pestle, so its six-inch diameter will make perfect contact with the granite slab's surface. Both the bottom of the muller and the slab have a slightly frosted finish, like ground glass, which accomplishes the grinding of the particles of pigment in the paste. As the workman slides the muller over the slab in wide, sweeping motions the film of color is gradually reduced in texture. At intervals, the workman scrapes up the mixture and redeposits it on the slab to further grind it until it attains the proper degree of fineness and consistency. This point is determined by spreading a very thin film of the color on a sheet of white porcelain and checking it by eye.

When I returned to the States I located some books on color manufacture and painting techniques. One, *The Materials of the Artist* by Max Doerner, a professor in the Munich Academy of Fine Arts, claims that modern color manufacturers using automatic grinding machines produced pigments of such fine consistency that they had a tendency to crack when used in painting. Another modern authority, Ralph Mayer, in *The Artist's Handbook*, disputes this idea. His book is a little later, and perhaps manufacturing methods had improved. However, Mayer does give explicit directions for the process of hand grinding, acknowledging that the artist will feel more in control if he can do the work himself. I was in sympathy with this conservative view and intrigued with the process. I liked the feeling of intimacy with the physical properties of paint, which I could control to some degree to suit my technique. I used a heavy glass grinding plate and a glass muller. Because my muller was not nearly as heavy as a granite muller of larger dimensions, it required a bit of strength to exert the required pressure. I felt considerable satisfaction in achieving what I felt, right or wrong, to be a superior result. Another advantage that most artists might be expected to applaud was the fact that the cost of my paints was much less than that of the best mechanically manufactured colors.

The first step in preparing the panels for the murals was to make the stretcher frames for the canvas. This was a process in which Bert was a great help. He made these in the college woodworking shop in three sections for easy assembly and portability. The top strip of the frame for the semicircular section of each panel was sawed from three-quarter-inch plywood. This section fitted into the well of the skylight when the panel was assembled and the canvas stretched thereon. The three main sections of each panel, made of three-quarter-inch by three-inch by one-inch poplar stock, measured approximately five feet by three and a half feet and were cross-braced for strength with the same stock material. When bolted together they made up the ten-and-a-half-foot-tall by five-foot-wide panels.

To stretch the canvas, each assembled frame was laid flat on low trestles that supported it on the sides. There were no supports on the ends. This allowed a slight sag in the frame along its lengthwise center and let us keep the canvas taut as it was stretched and tacked to the edge of the frame all around. The panel was then stood upright and secured in place under the skylight. It was given an oil ground consisting of one coat of cologne glue size and two coats of zinc white oil-base paint.

When this was dry, the next step was the preparation of the "cartoon," which is a full-scale pattern on paper of the outlines of all the elements in the design. This is a necessary aid to the muralist in enlarging the original sketch so that the design can be transferred to the canvas. To make this pattern, we covered the entire face of the canvas panel with strong wrapping paper of a brownish color. This came in a thirty-inch-wide roll that we cut into pieces thirty inches square, which we joined with transparent tape to make a sheet the size of the panel. The completed sheet was then taped to the panel at the edges.

The original sketch that had earned me the commission in the first place was now covered with vertical and horizontal lines forming one-inch squares. These were numbered along the left and right edges and lettered at the top and bottom. The paper on the panel was also lined, forming one-foot squares that were numbered and lettered to correspond to the one-inch squares on the sketch. This made it comparatively easy to duplicate the sketch at the enlarged scale while keeping everything in perfect proportion. Bert was all agog over this method of enlarging, which he had never encountered before. (Incidentally, the word *cartoon* was originally applied in this sense. Its modern use, applied to the comics, seems to derive merely from the fact that these are line drawings, as is the pattern used for murals.)

To transfer the design from the cartoon to the canvas, we perforated the lines of the cartoon with a "roulette," a small rotating wheel with sharp points on its periphery. It is mounted in a wooden handle and looks very much like a horseman's spur. The perforated lines were then gone over with a "pounce" bag—a small bag of porous cloth filled with a dark dry pigment. The dust of the pigment, filtered through the cloth of the bag, penetrated the perforations in the paper, leaving dotted outlines on the canvas. These were then made into continuous lines with diluted India ink on a fine-pointed watercolor brush.

Next came the underpainting, which established the color pattern in lighter, and sometimes different, colors from those planned for the final effect. In this I was lucky because Rannells had not required that I submit sketches in color for approval, as most mural patrons would have. I had explained that carrying out my sketches in black and white would allow me some spontaneity in the final painting, hoping everyone involved would approve, and I was very happy when this caused no problem. For my own reference, I made small, schematic color notes to use for guidance as I painted. This procedure gave me some of the freedom I so much desired. The underpainting was developed with pigments ground in linseed oil and thinned with turpentine. In this we were following the well-established practice of working from thin to thick coats and from light to dark tones to assure permanence of the final effect.

In composing these murals I owed a slight debt to Thomas Hart Benton, whose murals had attracted a lot of attention a few years earlier, and created some controversy among other artists. Benton's murals had helped to inspire a vision among some of a truly American school of painting called "regionalism." I did not subscribe whole-heartedly to this movement. I could not admire Benton's literal, almost commercial style, and I was also critical of his disregard for the architectural integrity of the interiors he decorated. Undeniably, however, he had the most admirable control of his medium and consummate knowledge of human anatomy. This allowed him to distort his figures to suit the undulating line of his style while still making them acceptable in his overcrowded compositions. He also innovated ways of including figures of different scale in whatever space was available. This was the one feature of his innovation that I utilized in my own compositions to separate elements of different scale and yet hold their components together as a whole. If, as I have heard, this proclaims me as an imitator or follower of Benton, so be it.

Several scenes of different scale were combined in each panel to convey the themes of recreation and labor, with the largest figures just over life-size. I did not use live models for my figures. In all my work, even portraits (after the one of Mrs. Curt Teich), I have painted people from memory or from very cursory sketches. In none have I striven for a photographic likeness as do the academic portraitists. And in the murals the figures are not realistic—they are all slightly romanticized or idealized, as is the whole concept.

One day as I was painting on the "Recreation" panel I heard footsteps entering the smaller room from the hallway. A rather pompous-looking man appeared in the doorway leading from the smaller room into the studio. He was portly, well groomed, and middle-aged. I thought he looked quite self-satisfied as I observed him from above on my scaffold while he scrutinized the painting without once looking at me. For some time he was silent; but at last he spoke—not to me, apparently, but to the world at large. In measured tones he said, "The hips on that girl in the square dance are much too large."

I laughed and replied, "Well, if that's a fault, it's one that's shared by an awful lot of women."

Without smiling, he introduced himself as Gordon Hall, a professor of economics at Eastern Kentucky State University in Richmond, fifteen miles north of Berea. He said he had heard about the murals in progress and come to have a look, as he was a great lover of art. He was obviously not impressed with my work; he was even slightly hostile. I refrained from saying the mural was nowhere near finished, thinking this might sound defensive. So we just talked briefly about the government providing employment for artists and let it go at that. Actually, after I thought about it, I decided this experience was encouraging. I saw it as evidence that even at this early stage, people were aware of the work going on and were at least somewhat interested, if only out of curiosity. I could imagine that in this small community everyone must know that something unusual was afoot.

Hall was just the first among several visitors who came to the studio during the painting of the murals. These visits helped a great deal in the process of my introduction to the community and of the community to me. I became acquainted with a good many interesting individuals who were to become close and lasting friends. Some were members of the college faculty; others were employees of the college's student industries; still others were students and townspeople who were just curious to see what was going on.

Among these visitors, I consider the most notable a young teacher in the college named Louis Smith. At that time he was a comparatively new addition to the faculty, teaching economics. A few years later he became dean of the college. Still later, his ability as an economist and his winning personality were recognized by the State Department when he was chosen to represent our government as goodwill ambassador to several foreign countries. On the day of his first visit he showed great interest in the mural; today, after these many years, he is still my dear friend and faithful correspondent. He has always had the most selfless devotion to the cause of Berea College: education of the underprivileged mountain people of Appalachia whom he loves so dearly. His students responded in kind to his devotion, and to his wonderful sense of humor, so that during his teaching years he was widely recognized as one of the most successful teachers in the nation.

Louis and I had much in common. We are both from Tennessee and are the same age within a few months; we were both on high school athletic teams and had similar youthful associations with rural mountain people. We also both enjoyed narrating anecdotes related to our early background and adding stories to our repertoires whenever we found them. Louis had accumulated a number in the course of his teaching. I remember in particular his telling about having casually mentioned to one of his classes that motion pictures were not developed until around 1900.

Immediately, a mountain boy named Luke jumped to his feet and said, "Why you know that ain't so, Mr. Smith! Don't you 'member jist last month you showed us that movin' pitcher of Dan'l Boone a comin' into the Kentucky wilderness? An' that was a long time afore 1900 you said."

Louis said this showed him up as a teacher. He supposed the rest of the class was just as puzzled as Luke, and it took him quite a while to straighten out the chronology of the historical events in their minds. (Remember, this happened in the early fifties. Undoubtedly Berea College students are much more sophisticated today.)

I now recall that as much as I enjoyed visitors there came a time in finishing the murals when I had to request privacy in order to concentrate fully. Everyone seemed to understand. Then, when they were at last finished, I let it be known that I would welcome all who might want to take a look before the paintings were taken to Lexington to be installed—and a good many responded.

During my work on what might be termed my first "public" murals, I had become well acquainted with the other occupants of the floor over the bank. They were among the first people Bert introduced me to on my first day in Berea, and they were perhaps the most frequent visitors to the studio. They also proved to be among the most interesting.

In two of the front rooms at the end of the hall that divided the top floor of the building, and immediately in front of the studio, was the office of the dentist Rube Gatliff. He was a very affable and likable man. His family had been among the earliest settlers in Madison County, and he had many relatives in the area. He was a mountain boy who had managed to get the education required to obtain a degree in dentistry and a license to practice. In spite of his comparatively advanced state of learning, however, he retained the idiomatic and ungrammatical peculiarities of speech of most of his associates. His "laboratory" contained a minimum of equipment, his waiting room a minimum of comfort. When he had no patient he was usually engaged in a game of checkers with one of his perennial adversaries in this intellectual pastime.

One of the recollections that remain clear in my memory is of entering his office one day when he was alone. I don't remember the reason for my visit; it was probably just to comment on the weather. It was a fine, warm spring day; the trees on the campus opposite the bank were just leafing out. Gatliff was standing in one of his habitual postures with one foot planted on the low sill of the tall, unscreened open window, gazing out at the world below. Without turning around to greet me he said, "Frank, you see that feller a-goin' along thar on t'other side of the street? That's Hiram Wilbe. He's got summa my teeth in his mouth he's had fer more'n a year an' they ain't paid fer nary speck."

"Well," I said, laughing, "I guess there's not much you can do about that is there?"

"Don't you think there ain't. I aim to wait my chance an' I'll do jist what I done to ol' Jeb Atkins a few years ago. He had a double plate of mine he'd owed me fer over a year. I ketched him a-settin' down out on the post office steps one day. He was a-jawin' right big to a couple o' fellers and didn't see me a-comin'. I stepped right afore 'im when he opened his mouth to say somethin' an' I reched in an' plucked them teeth right out. I put 'em in my pocket an I says t' him, 'You jist the same as stole them teeth from me an I'm a-takin' 'em back. Now as fer as I'm concerned you can jist gum it from now on.'"

I had to laugh, immoderately I fear. The doctor just glared. Then he said, "Hit may be funny to you, Frank, but when I spends my time, and my money fer materials, I don't aim to let nobody git by w'thout a-payin' me fer what they git. The only way he can git them teeth back is to come in like a man an' pay his bill." I agreed he was right.

On another occasion I was working in the studio when I heard an excited voice in the hall shouting "Far! far!" again and again. I dropped my brushes and ran to the door. I flung it open and there was Gatliff, running up and down the hall and shouting his quaint alarm. His features were contorted in an agonized expression of fear; then I noticed he carried his checkerboard under one arm as he ran. Behind him I could see the open door of his office. Beyond it the room was filling with smoke. I rushed to the phone in the studio and called the fire department at the station just around the corner on Short Street. Within minutes two student firemen were running up the long flight of steps from the street carrying fire extinguishers. They passed in through the smoke, and in no time the fire was out. It had originated in the wiring of the electric furnace in which the doctor burnt out the wax patterns he used in casting his dental inlays. The only damage was to the furnace itself and to the walls, blackened by the smoke.

I confess that I could not resist telling the story of the rescued checkerboard. It became a classic joke in the town. Luckily, I was not the only one who witnessed the doctor's concern for his recreational equipment, so I knew that if the story ever got back to him he would not know for sure who might have circulated it; he was hardly the type to appreciate a joke on himself.

On the other side of the hall from the studio, adjoining the dentist's office in front, was the apartment of Janie Carrington and her two boys, aged about seventeen and twenty at that time, I believe. Janie was a co-owner of the bank building with John Dean, cashier of the bank. Apparently there was a recurring argument between the two over details of the cost of maintaining the building overseen by Dean. This was well-circulated gossip in the town. Some wag with a scatological sense of humor had printed on the building's public toilet facility, "ALL TURDS WEIGHING MORE THAN TWELVE POUNDS MUST BE LET DOWN WITH A ROPE. SEE JOHN DEAN OR JANIE CARRINGTON FOR ROPE."

Janie, herself, knew all the gossip of the town; it was said she originated some of it on her own. She was more than willing to educate me in the moral turpitude and various other weaknesses of the local inhabitants. This was a most seductive facet of my orientation as a new member of the community. Of course I had to accept the information with certain reservations dictated by an awareness of the tendency of human nature to relay even the most questionable details as long as they are titillating.

When I was satisfied, as far as that was possible, with the final visual effect of the murals, I called Rannells, and he came to view them. Naturally, this was an anxious moment—"a moment of truth," if you will. So much had gone into my efforts, and so much depended on their effect on their patron, as well as their eventual effect on my career. Most important to me in the long run was to gain some recognition further afield than the local scene. Although I was not anxious to become known as a muralist, I hoped these panels might lead to an appreciation of what I considered my more legitimate work and to my eventual recognition as an artist.

To my relief, anxiety about Rannells's reaction proved groundless. He was clearly pleased with the murals and highly complimentary. He seemed sure the university president and Board of Regents would share his positive reaction and his belief that the murals could be counted on to reflect credit on the university.

He was also surprised that my work was finished so expeditiously. He said he had expected this commission to require a good deal longer. He intimated that he thought most artists working in a similar situation—that is, actually working for regular wages—would be inclined to try to stretch the work out to some nebulous time limit, since no firm one was set. The only comment I could think of was, "Well, possibly."

The first step in transferring the murals from the studio to their permanent location was to remove them from the stretcher frames and then disassemble the frames and pack everything ready for shipment to the university. The boxes were then sent to Lexington by truck freight.

Bert and I drove over the next day and went directly to the browsing room of the library, where the boxes were awaiting our arrival. We unpacked them, reassembled the stretchers, and restretched the canvases in the same manner as originally. Rannells had arranged for the university maintenance department to provide anything we might require and assistance in mounting the canvases in place.

On my first examination of the walls, before I began my work on the murals, I had discovered that the texture of the plaster was far too rough to allow me to cement the canvas directly to it—the usual method. The canvas would have to remain on the stretcher frames, which would be attached to the wall in toto. The slight sag that we had provided in our construction of the frames would allow for the expansion and contraction of the canvas under changing atmospheric conditions.

Under my instructions and supervision the university workmen raised and held each of the panels in turn flush against the wall in their positions at each end of the room. A two-foot-wide molding was placed around each panel and firmly attached to the wall, but not to the stretcher frame. Thus the whole panel was free to move the very slight amount needed for expansion and contraction within the surrounding molding. Now, after more than fifty years, it is gratifying to learn from university personnel that the canvases appear to remain always tight.

I was pleased with the amount of interest the murals attracted, both from the general public and from several critics in the arts sector. I continue to consider them my best murals in most respects, in spite of a number of faults of which I am well aware. The Lexington and Louisville newspapers had some flattering reviews, and the *Louisville Courier Journal* ran a reproduction in its rotogravure section. It was necessarily in sepia tones, since this was just a little before full color came into use for newsprint.

I was now happy to relax and enjoy a brief period of satisfaction over having created my first murals where they could be viewed by the general public. I felt sure that barring some disaster to the building they would exist for many years to come.

During the time I spent on these murals, and for some time thereafter, the other mural painted for the university under the PWAP program was being completed by Anne Rice (now Anne O'Hanlon). She had chosen to use true fresco as a medium for decorating a large wall space in a corridor of the new Memorial Hall. She elected to use this technique, a beautiful, ancient method of wall decoration, in spite of its exacting and time-consuming requirements, possibly because it is perhaps the most permanent of all mural media. Her renditions of various activities of the settlers of the Kentucky territory are extremely well designed and well executed. They owe a good deal to the style and execution of Diego Rivera, the famed Mexican political muralist of the time, and reveal the artist's delight in the medium she employed. As for permanence, even though my murals executed in oil on canvas show no sign of deterioration after more than fifty years, those done in true fresco, if undisturbed, could outlast by many times the building whose walls they grace.

CHAPTER 4
Back to Chicago, for a While

ALTHOUGH THE UNIVERSITY OF KENTUCKY murals were finished and there was nothing of a practical nature to keep me in Berea, I was in no hurry to leave. I enjoyed the experience of living in this new environment even more than I had expected to. I wanted to become more intimately acquainted with the community and the advantages I was sure it offered for an artist of my temperament. In addition, the fact that I could visit my parents whenever I chose made it more and more difficult to leave. So I stayed on in the studio for nearly a month, delaying leaving from day to day.

But of course the day arrived at last when I had to say good-bye to the several friends I had made there. They had begun to assume that I had become a permanent citizen of the town, since it was very obvious that I enjoyed living there. They knew nothing of my circumstances, and I think it was a surprise that I was planning to leave so soon after finishing the murals. Bert and Eva knew my situation, of course, but I think my leaving was an unforeseen disappointment to them too. Bert decided he would continue to rent the studio after my departure. He knew of my reluctance to leave and my hope to return. He seemed to be sure I would, although I could not see much chance of it in the near future, or in fact at any time I could foresee. In Lexington I spent a weekend with my parents before leaving for Chicago. I had gotten in touch with Dan Madsen, the friend who had kept some of my belongings for me when I left Chicago, and he had invited me to stay with him when I arrived—a gesture indicative of our warm friendship and his generous nature. I had already shipped back to him those items that I had been using in Kentucky.

During the first evening I spent with Dan, he had a most agreeable proposition for me. He said his erstwhile helper, another struggling artist, had left him a short time before, and if I wanted the job for a while he would be very happy, because he was badly in need of help.

Dan was managing to survive the depression by utilizing his artistic talent and knowledge of interior decorating to make a living, although he was actually a very accomplished painter. He had discovered a market in this field in the numerous nightclubs and speakeasies that were springing up to satisfy the demand for illegal liquor during the depression. This was a somewhat precarious source of employment, of course, since most of these places were either owned or dominated by gangsters. Dan seemed to have a knack for getting along with these characters and felt himself in no danger, but I had grave doubts about his safety.

On one occasion when he thought he might have trouble collecting his fee from some very questionable individuals, without his knowledge I carried my trusty automatic pistol to work. Fortunately there was no trouble. Dan was able to handle the matter with his characteristic poise and diplomacy and collected what was owed him with no difficulty. Later, I realized my foolhardiness and that I might have gotten both of us killed. It was the same rash, ill-considered impulsiveness that I had demonstrated through fear of the union when I was working on the Dubbs murals. When I thought it over, I was aware of my immaturity, and I believed I would never again be guilty of such a rash and stupid action. This was the era during which Al Capone and other gangsters dominated the Chicago underworld, and it was no time to become involved in anything they were interested in. Dan was simply lucky to have somehow won a kind of immunity in his business dealings with the fringes of that underworld.

Dan Madsen was a delightful Danish character who had come to America from his native island of Bornholm in the Baltic Sea when he was quite young. He was a few years older than I, but this was not apparent. The generosity previously mentioned was perhaps his most outstanding characteristic. He was constantly helping people less fortunate than himself out of their difficulties, particularly other artists. Among his many talents was a flair for carpentry, and it was this ability that had landed him in his location atop a small auto repair garage on East Ontario Street. He had become acquainted with the owner and charmed him into adding a second story to the building specifically to house Dan's studio-workshop-dwelling. Dan prepared the plans and completed most of the construction, adding a flower garden (he was an ardent horticulturist) on the upper level at the entrance to the studio. This combination formed a sort of oasis in the neighborhood, charmingly out of place among the modern buildings in the block. It seemed that other interests in the neighborhood had tried to buy this property occupied by the garage, but the owner was an eccentric individualist who enjoyed frustrating the would-be real estate tycoons.

The studio was roomy, and Dan would often give refuge to artists and the other new acquaintances he was always making. They might remain for periods ranging from overnight to several weeks. His harboring of me on this occasion was typical. During the time I was there, Dan also took in Charles Biederman, a young painter whom he found wandering the street in a daze, having been evicted from his room for nonpayment of rent. Another was George Elliot Perry, a middle-aged inventor struggling to perfect one of his numerous devices.

Charles was a very serious, no-nonsense painter, not long out of the Chicago Art Institute. He was determined to spend all his time painting, come hell or high water. He could not be persuaded to take a job and finally left to return to his hometown of Redwing, Minnesota. Years later he was sponsored by a wealthy art enthusiast and eventually achieved international recognition on a minor scale for his abstract constructions.

George Perry was the most eccentric man I have ever known. He was totally unaware of his eccentricity, even when tripping on his perpetually untied shoelaces. He was utterly obsessed with his vision of creating something useful that no one else had ever thought of. He was rather small, but his appearance was striking. He had cultivated a small triangular mustache, the apex of which pointed toward his upper lip, with the base under his nose. Its duplicate was on his chin. Between the two was as beautiful a set of gleaming white natural teeth as I have ever seen. He would explain that their perfection was due entirely to the use of his wonderful "tooth sticks." These were some kind of plant stems that he had impregnated with his wonderful tooth powder. About three inches long, the sticks had their ends cut off at an angle for easy contact with all tooth surfaces.

George had what most would consider a serious handicap to overcome. He was almost deaf in both ears to normal sound, such as conversation. He was a highly capable lip-reader, but in a day when battery-powered aids had just begun to appear on the market, he had a problem in carrying on a conversation with someone whose face he could not see. He designed his own hearing aid, which he wore on a cord around his neck. When in a situation where he was not facing his conversant, he would connect wires from the power unit into each ear. He could then hear perfectly, apparently. I asked him why he didn't patent the aid he wore. He replied that there were already aids on the market "almost" as good as his that were covered by patents. He simply was not interested in competing in this field. It was obvious that when he chose to invent, it had to be something needed that no one else had thought of.

He had several patents for commercially successful products. He invented the first time clock used by employees in industry to sign in and out at their jobs. It was called the "Perry Time Stamp." The flashing lights set up as danger signals on barriers at railroad crossings were another of his inventions. These lights are now used universally to mark traffic hazards during road and street construction and repair. With no wiring to a power source, they turn on automatically as daylight wanes. He had made a considerable amount of money over the years from these and other ingenious mechanisms, but with each invention he would sink most of the proceeds into financing the next—and not all of them were financially successful. When I knew him he was working on a process to clean hemp fibers of the plant material that surrounds them. In the metal "break" process universally used by the industry, the fibers are greatly weakened. George developed a special strain of bacteria that decomposed the material surrounding the fibers and literally devoured it without harm to the fibers themselves. He was also developing several in-genious applications for the cleaned and improved fibers.

For this experimental work he needed a relatively large laboratory. He had rented space on the top floor of a five-story building in the warehouse area. In the midst of his work he ran out of money and could not pay his rent or his electric bill. This did not faze him, although his electricity was cut off and his lab door locked. He was able to reach the roof of the building at night by climbing a fire escape ladder, and he could then enter the lab through a skylight. Once inside he had no trouble reconnecting the electricity and unlocking the door from the inside. A slightly larger problem was how to avoid being caught by the night watchman when he made his hourly inspections. George solved the problem by installing an on-off push-button switch under the tread of one of the stairsteps leading up to the top floor. He ran the concealed wire to the meter box. He had to do all this, of course, between the hourly rounds of the watchman. When everything was in place he could go to work at night without fear of being caught in the act. When the watchman came up the stairs and stepped on the activated tread, the light in the lab would go out and George could get out of sight before the watchman opened the door to shine his light inside. Seeing nothing, the watchman would descend the stairs, turning the lights in the lab back on when he stepped on the tread with the switch. George could then go back to work until the watchman's next round. Of course all this was both dishonest and illegal, but George was the soul of honesty and could be counted on to settle with the landlord and the electric company when his invention paid off. Right or wrong, we all felt he was justified by the circumstances, if not the law.

One of my most amusing recollections of my prolonged stay at Dan's haven for economically frustrated creators was of a Sunday outing that Dan, George, Charles, and I made to Dunes State Park on the Lake Michigan shore in Indiana. The trip was motivated by a desire to capture a landscape in that highly picturesque area. At least that was the motive of the others. I had already given up trying to paint from nature, finding that I could only *see* it after I had ceased looking at it. I went along for the ride, so to speak, though I may have hoped to store some mental impression that I might paint later.

There were only two bona-fide artists (besides me) on this excursion. George Elliot Perry was an impostor, according to the others of our party. But he had the conviction that he could do anything anyone else could do—not better, nor even as well perhaps, but differently. He had not been long rubbing elbows with us painters before he could not resist the urge to spend some of his valuable time as an artist. His unique approach was to do everything on a very small scale. His were not attempts to imitate the academic miniaturists; he was not interested in portraiture. He wanted to capture nature as seen through a reducing glass. I had to suspect that this impulse was inspired, if not completely motivated, by practical concerns, though he probably would have denied it. He had neither time, space, nor money to go into painting full-scale, so he went minuscule in a big way, so to speak.

Characteristically, he made his own equipment: miniature stretcher frames exactly like those of standard sizes, but hardly bigger than large postage stamps; miniature brushes fabricated using dowel pins for handles with carefully attached clusters of his own hairs and whiskers for the brush end. But none of his own hairs was fine enough for his thinnest lines. He told me gleefully that he had solved that problem by utilizing the incredibly fine fibers found in milkweed seedpods!

That Sunday we found the park contained its usual complement of weekend visitors and tourists. As each of my companions set up his easel and paint box in a different area before his selected view of the landscape, a group of onlookers would inevitably gather. This was an annoyance for Dan and Charles, but George loved it. A gregarious extrovert, he would beam at his audience, all of whom were showing far more interest in him and his paraphernalia than in Dan and Charles. And why wouldn't they? Everyone was intrigued to see what this little man was doing, crouched over a small folding table, which held a tiny easel, on which was an equally tiny canvas. They had seen other artists at work, but never one like this. As his painting gradually developed and neared completion someone would inevitably ask for a closer view. George would grin charmingly and hold it up for all to see. There would be questions, too, about his equipment and materials, which he would answer showing great appreciation for the questioner's interest. And when the painting was declared finished, there was always someone who would ask if it was for sale. The artist's face would light up like the Wrigley Building at night and he would ask, incredulously, "You want to buy it?" Then, after considering, he would ask, "Is five dollars too much?"

Actually, George painted some quite competent little landscapes that most people found very attractive. He had at least a modicum of talent, which he had never tried to develop because of his obsession with mechanics. He was able to complete one of these little pictures in an hour or less. He was the hit of the day, with a continually renewed and appreciative audience waiting to buy his modestly priced product.

In the car on the way home I was complimenting him on his success when Dan interrupted. He was indignant! "Those people who found your work so attractive are not art critics, George! You are no artist.

Why do you waste your valuable time on such foolishness as trying to be one. You should be satisfied with being a very talented inventor."

George was hurt. "Well," he said, "I guess you're right, Dan. The only thing is, I had a wonderful time, and I got some money! You and Charles may have had a wonderful time too. But you didn't get any money, did you?"

Then he laughed uproariously to cover up his hurt feelings, while Dan launched into a new critical tirade. I found the whole thing wonderfully funny.

I managed to get some painting done during this stay with Dan, but I was discouraged about the future. I didn't know how long I could continue believing I could someday support myself by spending all my time on the kind of painting I was sure my talent was capable of producing. If I had been alone, without friends, I doubt that I could have maintained my equilibrium. But I enjoyed my association with those I was living with and with a few other friends in the neighborhood. So I was able to quell those nagging doubts and continue to hope for some change for the better in my situation.

Then one day I got a letter from the U.S. Treasury Department that opened up a new vista—for the immediate future at least. It informed me that a new section of the department had been formed called the Section of Painting and Sculpture. (The name was later changed to the Section of Fine Arts.) Not very much information was given concerning the Section itself. The primary purpose of the letter was to inform me that under this program, designed to decorate new federal buildings with mural paintings and sculpture, one of the projects was for murals in a waiting room of the new Louisville, Kentucky, Marine Hospital. As a resident of the state, I was eligible to compete for a contract to execute the murals. The letter asked that I send for complete information and specifications of the spaces to be decorated if I was interested in competing.

At this point I must confess that until very recently I never knew any more about the Section than was told me at that time. I assumed its objective was primarily to offer employment opportunities for professional artists who had lost their patronage during the depression. This assumption was shared by everyone I knew, artists and laymen alike. It was a natural conclusion based on the fact that the other government art projects, as well as all other current public works projects, were funded under the National Recovery Act, President Roosevelt's solution to the economic disasters of the Great Depression.

The PWAP program under which I had done the murals for the University of Kentucky library expired shortly after that project was finished. It was abandoned in favor of putting artists to work under the auspices of the Works Progress Administration (WPA). WPA was a vast relief program that offered employment in almost every occupation—white collar, blue collar, and professional. The arts were among the last to be embraced—almost as an afterthought. These included not just the so-called fine arts but also music, drama, writing, and dance. Projects for these groups was confined for the most part to large metropolitan areas, where these arts normally flourished. Even Chicago lagged behind the large eastern cities. In Tower Town we had only vaguely heard of WPA for artists when I was working for Dan. I doubt that there was any such program there at the time.

To qualify for WPA projects one had to be practically destitute. This excluded the majority of the professionals. (It barely excluded me.) I found, however, that when I was working on murals for the Section everyone assumed I was doing them under the auspices of the WPA. Even today, it seems almost impossible to correct the impression that the WPA was responsible for all murals created during that period.

Looking back, I regret not having had a chance to paint during the depression under WPA's sheltering wing. In my financial condition I believe I might have found some way to fulfill the economic status requirement, and the conditions would have been perfect for me at that particular juncture of my life as an artist. Although the WPA paid only what was considered a minimum living wage (meager at best), it had many advantages for any serious artist wishing above all to perfect his style and technique and to pursue his career unhampered by the need to make a living by some other means.

I never heard of any complaints by artists on the WPA Federal Art Program, although there undoubtedly were some. There seemed to be so little to complain about—except the rate of pay perhaps, which was the same for everyone. For the most part, the production requirements were unbelievably lenient. The artist was required to produce only the amount of work he claimed represented his usual rate of production. There were few timekeepers and, strange as it may seem, there was not even a whisper about artistic quality. No government art critics ever came around to pass judgment on any WPA artist's work. This was exactly as it should be, of course, allowing perfect freedom for the artist in his creative efforts.

Rarely if ever has any government program designed to assist those in need been so free from self-defeating flaws. I have been told that this was not true of all the many other categories of projects under WPA. No doubt there were abuses, even in the arts division; but overall, WPA was an astonishingly successful effort on behalf of a substantial section of the economically suffering public. Several fine artists who took advantage of the opportunity later achieved prominence nationally and internationally. Jackson Pollack, the outstanding example among several others, laid the foundation for his career while working in the WPA Art Project in New York City.

Because the information I received about the Louisville project contained so little about the Section itself, I assumed it to be another effort by the government to expand its assistance of unemployed artists to include professionals who could not qualify under WPA. I was enthusiastic about it, of course. I am now both chagrined and somewhat amused by the fact that even though I worked for nearly ten years for the Section, it was not until recently that I learned the less-to-be-admired facts about its creation.

The goal of the Section of Fine Arts was not primarily to find work for artists. It was founded in October 1934 within the Procurement Division of the Treasury Department's Public Works Branch as the result of an idea shared by two rather unlikely individuals: Edward Bruce, a lawyer and painter, and Forbes Watson, an uncelebrated art critic. Rather than trying to solve the economic problems of the professional artists who had lost their patronage during the depression, Bruce and Watson had the grand idea of obtaining funding for an effort to lay the groundwork for a "truly American" school of painting.

Of course a depression is normally no time to expect government funding for any purely cultural project. Yet Bruce and Watson had influential political connections that made their dream of government support for their efforts to found a "truly American" school of art seem possible. In addition, they were able to make two persuasive arguments in favor of their idea of hiring professional artists to fill mural spaces in the new federal buildings being built all over the land. One was that 1 percent of each building's appropriation was being set aside for embellishment of some sort. The other was the fact that for most buildings, spaces where murals would be appropriate could be filled by this means at less cost than it would take to install the marble or granite facings normally used.

Bruce and Watson were both conservatives who believed American art was being unduly influenced by the radical "modern art" of the French schools of cubism and futurism and the other groups so much in the limelight of the day. Their sponsorship of a project to create murals in the many new federal buildings being constructed under the government's overall program furnished an excellent opportunity to promote their artistically conservative ideals. It is now obvious to nearly everyone that their ambition to found a new school of art was a failure, but economically the program was quite successful as far as the artists themselves and the public in general were concerned.

Bruce and Watson's rationale was that an American school should be established as a form of home-based illustrative art that they called "regionalism"—American artists concentrating on "the American scene," painting what they were familiar with, remaining "close to their roots." This trend had already been introduced by such muralists as Benton, John Steuart Curry, Reginald Marsh, and others, who took their cue from Mexican muralists such as Rivera and José Orozco, while avoiding the Mexicans' concentration on political themes. The American muralists saw the government mural program as a perfect outlet for their particular brand of talent, which was that of the illustrator. They seemed to consider this a sound basis for founding an indigenous national school of art. I am amazed at the audacity and conceit of the Section's founders in imagining that they could wield such influence on the American world of art. Of course they had the support of strong political influence in the highest offices in the land. President Roosevelt, charmed with their idea, gave it his complete approval.

The section was, incidentally, the very first agency of our government to be devoted to the fine arts exclusively—and it was temporary. Every other industrialized nation in the world had a permanent department in this category long before the United States did. It was not until 1965 that the permanent National Endowments for the Arts and for the Humanities were created by an act of the U.S. Congress.

The information I received from the Section did describe how the program operated. Competitions were periodically announced for mural and sculpture commissions to be installed in new federal buildings wherever the Section decided these were feasible and appropriate. There were three categories—local (state), regional, and national. Artists were eligible to enter if they had at any time been residents of the given area for five or more years. Those who applied were sent detailed information, including descriptions and dimensions of the space or spaces to be decorated and instructions for submitting designs. A list of acceptable subjects was given, but adherence to it was not required. Judging in national competitions was done by members of the Section. In regional and local categories, judging committees of qualified citizens were formed to make a rec-ommendation to the Section, which could accept or reject the choice.

I believe the competition for the Marine Hospital murals was a regional one. In spite of my apathy toward mural painting as an appropriate field for my talent, I decided to enter it. I had to think of my financial condition. I had no reason at all to believe I might win this competition, but I also could think of no reason why I should not give it a try with the best designs I might be capable of. I discussed this opportunity with Dan, and he encouraged me to make the attempt. I don't believe he quite understood my reservations about the mural medium.

I have only a very faint recollection of the designs I finally pro-duced. All I can recall is that the subject matter was Kentucky indus-tries and pursuits. At that time I had photos made of them, but these have long since disappeared. I remember only that the murals were for a quite small reception room in the hospital, and that the specified spaces completely filled all available surfaces except the ceiling. This presented a fairly difficult problem, as I recall it, but I believe I was reasonably well satisfied that my sketches were the best I could do. Of course my experience with murals was extremely limited.

I think it was at about this time that I discovered that monumental landmark of modern literature—James Joyce's *Ulysses*. I had always been a reader, and I was fascinated by the masterpieces of literary genius throughout history. This modern work utterly astonished me—as it has, and still does, so many others. A woman in the neighborhood who was a proofreader for some publisher or other had obtained a copy of the galley proofs of the book. Since it was still outlawed in the United States, no one seemed to know how she had obtained that copy, but she lent it to one of my friends who let me read it before returning it. I mention this here because, although I thought I could be nonchalant about the fate of my designs for the murals when I sent them off, I now recall that it was only while immersed in that utterly mind-absorbing book that I could suppress my anxiety over the outcome of the competition.

After what seemed an eternity of waiting, I at last received the letter from the Section. It informed me that, although I had not won the commission for the hospital murals, I was being offered a commission to execute ten mural panels in the new Federal Building in Louisville, provided I could submit suitable designs. The letter, from Ed Rowan, assistant to Edward Bruce, the program's director, was highly complimentary of my designs, but it explained that the Section felt I would be more successful working on an interior requiring larger-scale treatment than that provided by the Marine Hospital space. This, he said, was the reason for the alternative offer.

I was in a state of stunned but happy disbelief. Up to this point, my chances to survive as a painter had looked very dismal to me. Now, everything had suddenly changed. I could even look with some enthusiasm toward producing work with creative merit for this extensive and important commission. And I was sure it could be one more step toward recognition of my worth as an artist.

Once again I left my friends in Chicago with regret. But this was tempered by the anticipation of reestablishing myself as Bert Mullins's co-renter of the studio over the bank. The reunion would certainly be a happy one. In my most optimistic moments I had not dreamed that a return to Berea, which I had hoped for so strongly, would be possible so soon after I had left there. I also had a feeling that my recurrent struggles to survive in the Windy City were over, though I didn't know exactly why. For some quite illogical reason I had become very optimistic about the future. This feeling was buoyed up by the reception I received in Berea. There was no celebration; it was almost as if I had never gone away. It seemed that my eventual return had been fully expected, so there was no reason to treat it as a miracle.

I went to Louisville just the second day after arriving in Berea. I wanted to study the interior of the Federal Building and the spaces for the murals. I spent two days there, just wandering through the streets and along the waterfront of the Ohio River, further acquainting myself with the city, which I had not spent much time in before. This gave me a real feeling for its atmosphere and for what went on there. I did not have to do much research for the overall subject matter of the designs I would do for approval by the Section. They would be similar to those I had submitted for the Marine Hospital competition, but on a grander scale. I felt it unnecessary to work all of the designs out in great detail, but I did make an enlargement of one of the figures to indicate how fully the finished murals would be executed. I spent long hours for several days working the basic sketches out to my satisfaction, and I fervently hoped they would also be at least satisfactory to the Section. I wanted very much to get these approved so that work on the actual panels could start as soon as possible. They would be painted on canvas in the studio and cemented in place in the building when finished.

While I had been in Chicago a few things had changed. For one thing, my parents had moved from Lexington back to Knoxville to be near my brother, Joe, and his family. Both my father and my mother were showing signs of some of the ailments and frailties that usually accompany the aging process. Although they were in comparatively good health, they wanted to make this move as a precaution against any sudden illness that might occur.

Another alteration was that Bert was now spending most of his time in the studio. During my absence he had secured several commissions for paintings—enough to make him confident that he could now survive without his position at the college. I was pleased with his decision, feeling that I might have had a hand in preparing him for his independence. I felt certain his other talents would assure him of a job to fall back on if painting should fail to support him in the future. He wanted to resume sharing the studio and its expenses with me, but was content to use the smaller room and skylight for his own work. My work on the murals would of course require the larger space.

It was a day to be celebrated when I received word from the Section to go ahead with the Louisville murals. I had thought, with some dread, that alterations might be suggested, but there seemed to be complete satisfaction with my proposal. However, the letter from Rowan did present an unexpected development. It said that because of the extent of the project, I would need to hire two or three assistants through the WPA program in order to finish the contract within the specified one-year time limit, although this limit "could be extended if necessary."

I was taken aback by this maneuver—both surprised and somewhat disconcerted. I wondered then, and still wonder, if this seemingly unlikely requirement had ever been duplicated on any of the Section's other projects. I suspected that it might be just a convenient agreement with WPA to put more employees on WPA rolls. I had never worked in the capacity of boss over other artists and had no idea of how I could utilize help on this project. But of course I had no choice but to comply.

As was suggested, I returned to Louisville to confer with Adele Brandeis, the wife of the famous Louis Brandeis, then a justice of the Supreme Court. She was the overall supervisor of the WPA Federal Art Project in Kentucky. This gracious lady invited me to her home to confer, and we talked at length about the Louisville project. She was familiar with some of my work and said she was delighted that I was to do the murals for the Federal Building. She gave me information on how to go about obtaining the assistants required through WPA.

The next step was to proceed to the WPA office in downtown Louisville. The staff there had been notified of the job opportunities associated with the murals and had searched their rolls for possibly qualified personnel. They had only two for me to interview. The first was a personable young lady, Marian Myers, who had been working in a commercial art studio before the depression. She had had limited experience with the oil medium to be used in the murals, but I had hopes of her being able to follow my directions in preliminary work on the murals well enough.

The other was a surprise. He was Alois Ulrich, a little man in his seventies. He had emigrated from Germany to this country, with his family, when he was in his twenties and had been working for a commercial art firm. I was doubtful that he could be of much assistance on the murals since his specialty was pen and ink. But I was willing to do my best to help him to become a satisfactory helper on the murals. He was a most interesting little man, full of laughter bubbling through a thick German accent. He was enthusiastic about the chance for a job with a "real artist."

One of our interviews was in his home. He was living with his daughter and her family in a crowded little house on the outskirts of town. It was obvious that they were on the borderline between poverty and self-sufficiency. But they seemed very happy to all be together and that "grandpa" was to have a job again. I was embarrassed at the role of benefactor they insisted on assigning to me over my protests. I would have had a hard time rejecting Alois if it ever came to that.

After returning to Berea, I began a search for living quarters for the two assistants to consider when they should arrive in the next few days. All this I discussed with Bert, of course. In the course of our conversation I was surprised when I discovered that he would like very much to also become one of the assistants. Since Rowan had specified "two or three," this did not seem totally impossible, although Bert appeared to be doing fairly well on his own. I had not considered the possibility previously because he was not certified for WPA employment, and I was not sure he could be. He didn't know either, but thought it possible. On investigating I found that the local WPA office could make the certification if Bert could qualify, but an application would have to be reviewed by the office in Louisville. That would mean another trip to Louisville, this time with Bert. With the preliminaries out of the way, we made the trip to see Mrs. Brandeis and convince her of Bert's qualifications, which was surprisingly easy to do.

It was not long after this that Alois, Marian, Bert, and I were all working harmoniously together in the studio, preparing the canvases for the first of the murals. Because of space limitations, it was not feasible to prepare all the canvases at once, which would have been more efficient. We had to do a few at a time, stretching the canvas on the frames, then applying the glue sizing and ground coats to the raw canvas, as Bert and I had done for the University of Kentucky murals. The assistants could carry out this work without my supervision while I was busy finalizing the working sketches preliminary to doing the

The Louisville Federal Building murals. Courtesy National Archives.

The Louisville Federal Building murals. Courtesy National Archives.

cartoons. Bert oversaw their work during this stage and also during the preparation of the cartoons, since he was familiar with these steps from the Lexington murals.

Of the ten panels, four were "lunettes" (half circles) to go in spaces over the elevator doors. Each of these measured approximately three feet and four inches high by nine feet wide. Two of the panels were for alcoves flanking two large main lobbies at opposite ends of the building. The remaining four panels were for the lobbies themselves. Each of the latter rooms would have two panels the same height as the two alcove panels, but twenty-five feet long. These dimensions are approximate, materializing out of my less than perfect memory of these details after so many years. At least they give an idea of the size and proportions of the spaces. The very long panels were difficult to compose with all elements relating in a way that avoided any static or monotonous effect. The scale of the figures had to be as large as possible because of the distance and the angle from which they would normally be viewed when in place. The compositions were carefully controlled in the sketches to avoid any monotony, then were enlarged by the grid system to full scale in the cartoons, whose outlines were then transferred to the canvas.

Marian Myers and Alois Ulrich were now both well situated and adjusted to living in Berea. They really seemed to be enjoying their work and their new surroundings. I found with great satisfaction that after the first group of panels the basic procedures could all be satisfactorily carried out by them. I was glad indeed that Bert had become one of the crew and could supervise the preliminary procedures without my help. This made it possible for me to work on several easel paintings during this period.

CHAPTER 5
Life in Berea

W ITH THE START OF THE LOUISVILLE MURALS my
"settling-in" process in the Berea community began. Almost
unconsciously, I began to believe that this would be my home for
a long time to come. This was illogical, of course. My belief was
based on youthful optimism that disregarded the fact that I had
only temporary gainful employment and no assurance whatever
that after this commission was finished there would be any further
opportunities. At any rate, the specter of being unable to continue
to pursue a career in art, which had haunted me for so long, was
no longer lurking in the recesses of my mind, whether its absence
was justified or not. It could be said that my new freedom from
worry about the future allowed me to become preoccupied with the
mural project.

At the same time, it allowed me to become engrossed in learning
about this comparatively new environment, of which I had barely
had a taste while working on the University of Kentucky Library
murals the year before. I was able to renew all the acquaintances I
had made then and to add many more. Bert continued his assistance
with this process, and it was not long before I began to have the
feeling that I was becoming accepted as a full-fledged citizen of the
town. I soon discovered that while Berea was quite similar in some
ways to other small college towns in Appalachia, it was unique in
several respects. Naturally, the fact that Berea College is a unique
institution among small colleges had a great deal to do with creating
a sense of difference in the town itself.

The layout of the town is also a part of what makes it different. It
is situated on a long ridge of land, a part of the foothills of the Cumberland Mountains, which continue to rise up toward the eastern
boundary of Kentucky with the Virginias. The first settlement was
on the relatively flat top of this ridge; and since the first settlement
included the college, it grew in this area and became the nucleus
of the town. Business and residential areas were gradually added on
the ends rather than on the sides of the ridge, because these sloped

away rather steeply. The additions became known as the east and west ends. A local character once said of the town, "Hit's like a pair-a saddlebags throwed acrost a mule's back."

My studio over the Berea Bank and Trust Company was on the block-long Main Street, which separated the east end of the town from the college campus. This was the east end's main business street, the only other being Short Street, which paralleled Main at the rear of the bank.

Main Street housed several businesses along its one-block course. These began on the north end with a soda fountain and newsstand, which was also the Greyhound Bus Station. The whole enterprise was operated by T. P. Baker and his wife. If you were standing across the street from the bank with your back to the college campus, this emporium would be on your left at the corner of Estill and Main. To the right of it was the entrance to the long staircase leading up to the floor over the bank and our studio. To the right of the staircase was the facade of the bank itself, with an extensive plate-glass window on which letters in gold leaf proclaimed the bank's name and its capital assets of $50,000.

In this connection I shall always remember fondly one of my newly made friends named Greenberry Angel, who had a wonderful suggestion. "What you'd orta do, Frank," he said, "is git you some cards printed up with FRANK W. LONG, ARTIST on the top line—then under that, Ass sets over $50,000."

My sense of humor urged me strongly to act on this tantalizing concept, but realizing that this would seriously threaten my acceptance by the town's elders, I reluctantly gave up the idea. The bank's impressive window also served as a display case for its president and several of the major stockholders. On most any good day they might be seen posing for public view in comfortable chairs, gazing out proprietorially on the passing citizenry, many of whom depended on the institution in all financial matters.

Next to the bank was the Porter-Moore Drug Store, and on down the street, separated only by stairways to their second floors, which housed mostly offices of the town's doctors and dentists, were successive business enterprises. These included a dress shop, a men's clothing store, another soda fountain and sandwich shop, a photographic studio (the one that had vacated the studio over the bank), the Berea College Cooperative Store, known as the Coop Store, and finally, on the corner at Chestnut Street, Boone Tavern, owned and operated by the college. The Tavern was, and is still, widely known as a high-quality hotel, patronized by discriminating travelers from far and wide. Incidentally, the title *Tavern* is something of a misnomer, at least to those who interpret it to indicate the availability of alcoholic beverages—heaven forbid! I believe its official name is Boone Tavern Hotel, which is somewhat redundant of course, but apparently deemed necessary to help avoid any such confusion. The hotel is a Georgian Colonial structure with an imposing facade of a broad veranda and towering columns supporting the upper stories. It completes the block-long front edge of the east-end business district.

The hotel and some of the other buildings extended clear through to Short Street, the one-block-long street immediately behind and parallel to Main. Here there were other businesses in buildings along both sides of the street. There were two shoe repair shops, two cafés, a dry cleaner's, a real estate office, and a sewing room operated by Berea College. On part of the far side of the street was the two-story Boone Tavern Annex, providing rooms rented by the month to more or less permanent guests.

I soon became acquainted with the personnel of all these enterprises and a patron of most. I remember particularly with pleasure the remarkable personality of Frau Fish, who owned and operated Little Mama's Café on Short Street. She had been a German citizen in Berlin when she met Grover Fish, a Berea boy, while he was serving there in the American army during World War I. They married, and she came to Kentucky with him at the end of the war. They had an apparently happy life together until Grover died, not long after the younger of their two boys was born.

The café was quite successful, due not so much to the cuisine as to little mama's irresistible charm. Her heavy accent and originality in restructuring the English language caused great good-natured amusement to the locals, who of course were never aware that their own vernacular was just as strange to other Americans from outside their sphere. But accent was not all that attracted her patrons; she had that rare quality of being obviously and sincerely interested in anyone she might meet, not only in the café, but anywhere else.

Then there was Dr. Alson Baker, whose office was over the drug-store. He was a longtime friend of Bert's, and it naturally followed that he became one of my first acquaintances in the neighborhood. We soon discovered that we had a common interest in literature and pleasure in discussing it. The doctor was uncommonly well ed-ucated among the locals, but he retained some of the characteristics that marked so many of those with a similar early background. He normally spoke very good English. When he spoke in the vernacular it was with tongue-in-cheek humor and a self-deprecating smile—unless he was excited; then he lapsed into the local language un-consciously. Another of his interests was in firearms. This he shared intimately with Bert. They seemed almost obsessed with a fascination for pistols. I soon learned that Bert carried a concealed forty-five-caliber Colt revolver almost constantly, and he very early took me in hand to teach me the fine points of handling and shooting a pistol. Although I had always been interested in guns and in marksmanship, I had never had any particular interest in handguns. At first, I was only mildly curious about my new friends' interest, but it soon began to seem a little excessive for a purely innocent hobby. Then I discovered that almost all of my new acquaintances had this same preoccupation. I also learned it was a well-known statistic that throughout eastern Kentucky at least 90 percent of the male descendants of the early settlers carried handguns as a matter of course. This practice is a carryover from the early days of the family feuds of Appalachia, some of which have refused to die out.

In due time I learned that Bert, when quite young, had been acquitted of killing a man in a gunfight. No details were offered by my informant, except that the verdict in a court trial had been self-defense. In fact, my informant acted a little as if he regretted having let this story slip out, and it was never mentioned to me by anyone else. But to me, this account went a long way toward explaining both Bert's odd fascination with pistols and his conflicting emotions about the act of killing, which were revealed to me at about the same time. Finally, I learned—from Dr. Baker himself—that the Baker family had been nearly wiped out in a famous feud in Clay County, Kentucky, in the very early days of the doctor's youth. This, he explained with a sardonic smile, was why he was practicing medicine in Madison County.

I cannot remember being particularly shocked or intimidated by the revelation of such a militant undercurrent in this segment of the population in the area that I now considered my new home. As far as I could tell, there was no reason to believe that violence might break out at any moment. I followed my usual optimism in believing that what had existed in the old days was probably no longer a threat. Besides, with my no-doubt-congenital interest in firearms, it was no problem for Bert to enlist me into the ranks of the pistol shooters. I acquired a thirty-eight-caliber Colt revolver and enjoyed frequent practice sessions with Bert, and occasionally with Dr. Baker. Bert finally suggested that I carry the pistol regularly and concealed, as he did, saying, "you never know what might come up."

I had always been a good shot, but I could never equal Bert in the off-hand shooting on which he concentrated. This was in the tradition of the old West—that of the gunslingers—and involved drawing and firing from the hip at a preselected small target while walking down a path in the woods. This seemed to me to have lethal implications.

Coupled with my interest in the gunslinger phenomenon was my curiosity about why Bert always seemed to avoid any discussion of using his marksmanship in hunting for game. I had been an avid hunter all my early life, following in the footsteps of my sportsman father. One of the things I had missed most when I left home for study in Chicago was having an opportunity to roam the woods and fields in search of game. I had been elated over what I envisioned an opportunity to renew this pursuit in the Berea setting. I had anticipated that Bert would act as guide and companion in hunting the small game that I knew was abundant in this part of Kentucky. At last I brought up the subject directly by asking him if he never went hunting. He was very hesitant in answering but finally tried to explain. He said that he simply could not bring himself to kill a defenseless animal. He was careful to avoid criticizing those who liked to hunt, seeming to imply that this was just an idiosyncrasy of his which he had had all his life. As he warmed up to his explanation he told of having gotten into a fight once, as a twelve-year-old boy, when he came on two of his classmates torturing a tumblebug!

This was a revelation that gave me much food for thought. It seemed to me it could only mean that Bert was suffering from a deep-seated emotional conflict. By killing a man, even though it was to save his own life, he had violated his instinctive horror of killing as an act in itself. Although he was uneducated in the Hindu religion, he had the same respect and regard for all forms of life that characterize that religion. But his feeling was entirely instinctual—not philosophical. In this he might be classed with the famous Dr. Albert Schweitzer, who would avoid harming even an insect no matter how annoying it might be.

But Bert was steeped in the tradition of the blood feud—"an eye for an eye"—and felt he had to be prepared to uphold his "honor" at any cost. This combative readiness was sharpened by his sense of inferiority when he compared himself to the more educated, more sophisticated people with whom he came in contact. This sense of inferiority was seldom revealed except when Bert was intoxicated; then it came out in all its ugliness. In these episodes, he would become overbearing and domineering, sometimes ordering a passing stranger to continue on his way without looking back. This attitude of course was backed up by his feeling of superiority established by the pistol he carried. It was remarkable that he did not get embroiled in more trouble than he did. It seemed sometimes that the town itself had become tolerant of Bert's transgressions.

As I became more aware of this facet of Bert's character, I was surprised that it had never threatened to our friendship. I was never the victim of his drunken, aggressive behavior. I cannot deny that we were sometimes drunk together. On those occasions I was careful to remain less intoxicated than he, and I found that he was willing to listen to my counsel about the advisability of relative sobriety. At times I would resort to the ruse of hiding the bottle and claiming I could not remember where it was. Bert's father was surprised at my influence, saying I was the only person who had ever been able to "handle" Bert. I had to attribute this to Bert's consuming desire to become an artist and to his seeing me as a friend and a guide who could help him realize his ambition.

There was one occasion that honesty compels me to include in these confessions, as it reveals something significant not only in Bert's character, but also in my own. It occurred one late summer afternoon as he and I were walking along Chestnut Street through the west end of town. He had invited me to supper with him and Eva at their home on the town's outskirts. We noticed a number of factory-new pickup trucks parked in a line along the curb of the street. A group of several men stood at the end of the line; apparently these were the drivers of the trucks, which were being delivered from their origin in one of the auto plants in northern Ohio to dealers all along U.S. Highway 25 to the south. This was a common sight in Berea, and this shady street was a favorite spot for the drivers to take a break and have a smoke with their buddies. Bert and I were having an animated conversation as we passed by. Bert was speaking rather loudly in the local vernacular, and this seemed to draw the attention of at least one member of the group. He called out in a loud voice as we passed, "Hey, fellers. Do you know where a feller can find a feller that knows a feller that'll help a feller shuck a feller's corn?"

The insulting assumption that we were stupid yokels was only too apparent. Several of the group were snickering. We halted, staring back at the man, who was grinning. Bert was of course carrying his trusty firearm under his coat. I was also carrying mine the same way. After a long moment, Bert replied, "Well, from the number of damn fools I see standin' aroun' hyur I don't think you'll have a bit of trouble afindin' one, mister."

I was as angry as Bert. I felt compelled to back him up. I put in a warning, "The next time you idiots come through here, you'd better keep your damned mouths shut."

We all glared at each other. A local boy standing by who seemed in his early teens broke the silence. He yelled out, "Well, they told you didn't they mister, an' you better listen to 'em, man. You're in Kentucky now. You cain't git away with that kinda shit aroun' here."

There was dead silence as we walked away. It was obvious that the audience had gotten the message. No doubt they knew the reputation of Kentucky mountaineers for violence and about the prevalence of firearms.

As I have thought about it in later years I have not been proud of my role in the affair. The proper course for us would have been to walk on as if we did not hear the insult. Our resentment had brought us close to possibly tragic consequences. But one does not break away from traditional behavior easily. And Bert obviously appreciated the role I had assumed in backing him up. This was a perfect example of what he had in mind when he persuaded me to carry a pistol.

Bert's comparatively mild alcoholism never interfered with his work in the studio, and progress on the Louisville murals was very satisfactory to me. Apparently the Section of Fine Arts was satisfied with my reports as well. The underpainting, carried out by the assistants with my instruction and supervision, was proceeding well. We worked on the smaller panels first, allowing the apprentices to learn to produce the effect I desired in the underpainting before moving on to the larger canvases. Although the first panel or two went very slowly, I could not foresee any difficulty in eventually finishing the whole project within the specified time. I was particularly pleased to find time to also work on other paintings more agreeable to my talent.

During this period, although I seemed to be receiving significant kudos as a "regional" painter in the competitive exhibitions I entered, I was not very pleased with this classification. It may have been applicable to some of my work, but I was more pleased with other paintings that I considered far more original. Even so, I had to admit to myself that I felt I was slipping unconsciously into the "regional" category. I was convinced that most of the work being produced under the artificial stimulus of a government mural program—which necessarily required an emphasis on subject matter over aesthetic excellence, and relied on the artists' financial need for their participation—consisted of mere illustrations that were predictably of widely varying quality. Because of my conviction that this was true, I could not be greatly pleased with my own mural work. Although I enjoyed much of what I created other than the murals, there was often the nagging feeling that I was missing the true direction I had hoped to find. Even so, I was managing quite well to enjoy my life as an artist in the kind of congenial atmosphere the Berea setting afforded, in spite of my largely philosophical discontent.

It was at this point that the well-known photographer Doris Ulmann came to Berea on her project of depicting the people of the Appalachian Mountains and their customs. She was an independently wealthy artist, practicing her art without concern for its financial success. She used the most expensive equipment, materials, and techniques, and her prints were processed by a phototechnician in New York City, which was her home base. Unfortunately, she was in ill health and unable to travel and accomplish her work without assistance. It was lucky indeed that she had been able to form a close working alliance with the American folklorist and musician John Jacob Niles, who was interested in collecting early American folk music in the same area. He agreed to travel with her and assist physically with her work while gathering material for his own project. His *Ballad Book of John Jacob Niles* is now recognized as a very important work on the subject of the Appalachian Mountain folk ballads, brought to America by the early settlers from the British Isles.

One morning there was a knock on my studio door; when I opened it, John Jacob (or Jack, or Johnnie) Niles appeared. He stuck out his hand and proclaimed in dramatic fashion that he was John Jacob Niles, no less! He looked over my shoulder, saw the nearly finished painting in progress on my easel, slapped his forehead, and exclaimed, "My God! That's GREAT! How much for all night?"

My imperfect memory suggests the painting might have been any one of several that eventually went into Johnnie's collection of my work. Anyhow, he bought it on the spot, to be delivered when finished in the next day or two. This incident was typical of Johnnie; he was impulsive, egotistical, ebullient, dramatic—a showman who captivated audiences worldwide with his renditions of the plaintive folk songs of Appalachia.

After discussing the painting and his enthusiasm for it, he went on to explain why he and Doris Ulmann were in town and the fact that she had heard about my studio and its skylights. She wondered if there might be a chance that I would agree to let her use it for an hour or so on one or two occasions to photograph individuals for her project, which he explained at length as well as talking about his own. I agreed, of course, and learned that Bert's consent had already been obtained.

Thus began my friendship with Johnnie Niles, which lasted for the rest of his long and productive life. Ending so regrettably in 1980 when he was at the age of eighty-seven, his was a life duly celebrated by his recognition as a foremost authority, collector, recorder, and performer of early American folk music. Unfortunately, he had his detractors. Some claimed he was guilty of collecting some of his "discovered" folk songs out of his own head. One of his most famous, "I Wonder as I Wander," which he claimed was initially sung to him by a mountain girl in the small town of Murphy, North Carolina, has never been "discovered" by any other expert on American folk music.

It is a paradox that what is meant as a bitter indictment, if viewed in another light, is an unintentional tribute to his overwhelming musical talent.

In the early thirties, Johnnie was living in New York City; but he returned to the Appalachian area a year or so later with his bride, Rena Liepetz, for eventual permanent residence on the bluegrass farm they bought near Lexington. He was a native Kentuckian, having been born and raised in a rural section near Louisville called "The Cabbage Patch." Rena was the daughter of a well-known Russian inventor and scientist and his wife; they had fled that communist country to the United States not long after Rena was born.

Johnnie was already celebrated in the region for his music and other accomplishments, and it was not long before the Niles home became a center for informal social gatherings of people in the arts, including several from the University of Kentucky's art and music departments. Some were old acquaintances of mine, including Henry Warder Rannells and several members of his staff. I remember in particular Clifford Amyx and Raymond Barnhart. Ray, now a resident of California who has gained a great deal of recognition for his sculptural constructions and assemblages of found objects, became a lifelong friend. I also cemented my friendship with the Nileses during this time. Johnnie and I had very similar tastes and interests. For a couple of things, I admired his music, and he admired my paintings. There is nothing like mutual admiration to cement a permanent friendship.

I spent many evenings and some weekends with the Nileses in Lexington, and on occasion we got together in my studio in Berea, where Johnnie would usually sing some of the ballads from his growing repertory, accompanying his voice, which was of a highly unusual timbre, with music from a dulcimer. This could be any one of several instruments that he had made, depending on the key in which the song was written. (The key of the dulcimer itself cannot be changed to accommodate that of the song.) This meant that when performing publicly he would have to have several instruments at hand on the stage, but usually not more than three. In making these instruments, Johnnie was meticulous in his craftsmanship and highly creative in his designs. Normally, he did not stick to the two or three traditional designs of the mountain craftsmen. He often experimented with designs based on the lute and other stringed instruments, ancient or modern.

I became engrossed in the study of Johnnie's unique personality. According to both himself and many friends, he was undeniably an egotist of the first water. He would brag shamelessly about his own talents and accomplishments; yet at the invitational parties in his home he was the most gracious of hosts. If a guest had some special ability, or had achieved something special, he would be sure to call it to the attention of the company; or if he knew someone had a particular talent to demonstrate, a good story, or an interesting experience to relate, he would always give him or her an opportunity to perform for everyone's benefit and their own gratification. In spite of his egotism, he did not deny anyone else's right to his or her own brand. No wonder his parties were always so successful.

Rena also had this talent to a marked degree. She was a perfect wife for Johnnie, sharing his tastes, his interests, and his inclinations. She had considerable writing talent and soon became a feature writer for the *Louisville Courier-Journal*. I felt fortunate indeed to have made two such friends: first, because of my genuine affection for them, and second, because they proved to be so influential in promoting my career as a painter. They introduced me to several prospective patrons in Kentucky from their wide acquaintance, and Rena, from time to time, wrote reviews and feature stories in the *Louisville Courier-Journal* and the Lexington papers about my work.

Meanwhile, the Louisville mural was still progressing to my satisfaction. Bert was able to work on his own projects to a satisfactory degree in the spare time after our work on the murals. Most of his energy was spent on the prodigious task he had set for himself in building a native-stone house not far from his original family home on Clear Creek near Disputanta. It would be his and Eva's new home and his studio. The other two assistants both seemed to be enjoying their work. Both had made friends and appeared to have fitted easily into the community.

Alois Ulrich was a devout Catholic. He had some difficulty practicing his religion as assiduously as he wanted to, since the nearest Catholic church was in Richmond, some fifteen miles away. But very soon he made friends with the nurse who assisted Dr. John Baker in his office, and this solved most of his transportation problem. She had a car and she was a Catholic. She had become one of Alois's new friends and was glad to have him accompany her to mass.

But inevitably there came a weekend when Cathy, the nurse, went to visit her family in Louisville. Alois was frantic. He asked my friend Chester Parks to lend him his car for the trip to early mass. He did not ask me, knowing I did not own a car, and no doubt thinking I might refuse even if I did. Of course he felt somewhat in awe of me as his employer. But he had become acquainted with Chester and knew him to be an accommodating type. Chester was surprised. He asked Alois if he knew how to drive—a natural question in view of Alois's age and rather decrepit condition. Alois answered, "No, but if you vill chust zhow me how, it vill be all-right. I am a very fast learner."

Naturally, the course of instruction in driving never took place. Alois finally became resigned to missing the mass and reasoned that he would not be subjected to utter damnation because God would know he had tried his best and that his lapse was unavoidable.

He was a very lovable old man whom everyone enjoyed talking to and listening to. This was the period of the rise of Hitler to power in his native Germany, and he became Alois's hero. In this, he was strongly influenced by the radio broadcasts of the notorious Father Coughlin, a Canadian Roman Catholic priest whose reactionary views were published in his magazine, *Social Justice*, to which Alois subscribed. People in Berea had not yet formed very clear ideas on this subject, which was fortunate. Alois's sentiments were never seriously challenged as far as I knew, and of course I scrupulously avoided even mentioning the subject to him.

In spite of his misdirected patriotism, Alois was an amusing little man who was always getting into embarrassing situations caused by the forgetfulness typical of many in his age bracket. On one occasion he was frantic over having lost the paycheck he had just received in the mail. A general search of the studio was instituted and carried out by all hands. In the midst of the hunt Alois suddenly called out in sheepish embarrassment. He had located the check, stuck in the inner sweatband of his hat, where he had apparently hidden it until he could get it cashed.

As an artist, he actually had very little talent, but at his previous job it had been enough to provide a minimal living for himself and his family. That work seemed to have consisted of copying decorative borders and other embellishments, designed by other artists for book illustrations of various kinds. At least that was what he had been doing immediately before he became unemployed and was selected for our mural project. No doubt he had done other types of artwork that I never learned about. He was not very adaptable to the kind of painting we were doing, as he had never worked in oils, but with careful supervision his assistance was at least adequate, and I was glad to be the source of the employment he needed so much. He soon developed an excessive admiration for my work and my abilities. It was most embarrassing when he would insist to everyone that I was an "abzolude cheenius" who would be recognized as a great artist in time.

My reports to the Section of Fine Arts of work in progress on the murals were apparently satisfactory, but after several months I was notified that a representative would soon visit the studio to inspect them. Apparently this was a routine requirement of the Section on projects of this size, and I was glad of an opportunity to show the work, even in its incomplete stage, to someone presumably competent to judge it. I remember that when the representative appeared (a young man whose name I cannot now remember), I was disillusioned when he explained that he only wanted to make sure that a satisfactory amount of work had been accomplished up to that point—he was not interested in the artistic quality of the work, but apparently just in the number of square feet of canvas that had been covered! It seemed this was following some regulation imposed by the fact that my assistants were being paid what amounted to a salary by WPA. But the young man was pleasant enough and agreeable enough for us to enjoy his visit. He seemed impressed by the physical progress of the work during the time that had elapsed and expressed his apparently unrequired personal opinion that it was of the highest aesthetic quality. There seemed no reason to feel the slightest concern over what his report to the Section might reveal or how it would be received. At this point I felt reasonably well pleased with the way the murals were progressing toward completion.

CHAPTER 6
Hunting and
Other Diversions

VERY SOON AFTER STARTING the Louisville project I began to spend some of the time I could spare in the fields and forests within a few miles of Berea. I bought a twenty-two-caliber rifle equipped with a three-power scope sight for squirrel and rabbit hunting. I would often be in the woods before daylight during the squirrel season and was usually very successful in finding and bagging the elusive gray and the less numerous fox squirrels. Sometimes I would have a companion hunter—one who shared my ethics and tastes in hunting exclusively with the rifle, rather than the shotgun favored by most of the native hunters. I wanted the satisfaction of a clean kill—a shot to the head—with no risk of wounding the animal to suffer a lingering death. This usually required expert stalking to obtain a clear shot at the animal. With the telescope sight, successful shots could be made at greater distances and with better accuracy than with the ordinary iron sights.

I was very conscious of the difference in Bert Mullins's and my attitudes toward hunting, and at times it disturbed my equanimity when I allowed myself to think about it. I had to feel a certain admiration for Bert's compassion, and perhaps a latent sort of shame that I could not share his depth of feeling to the point of sacrificing my love of hunting. I would remember certain moments in my experience when what might be thought of as my better instincts won out and I had given up a clear opportunity to make a kill. Once, when I had had a clear shot at a young squirrel, his brother appeared and they began to play, wrestling with each other on a broad limb with such obvious fun and joie de vivre that I could not pull the trigger. And there were a few other instances of like nature, which revealed my inherent tenderheartedness. But it was not until many years later in arctic Alaska that I awoke fully to a reverence for all living things and an understanding of the depth of Bert's struggle with the contradictions between his nature and the facts of his life.

I was with a group of Eskimos on a caribou hunt. They had invited me to go along when the great herd came within forty miles of their village in its winter migration—near enough to make the hunt practical from a logistical standpoint. A small part—three or four hundred—of the main herd of many thousands had been located the night before, bedded down in a small valley in the low hills. We left our nearby overnight camp well before full daylight (about noon in December in the arctic) and climbed the backside of one of the hills. We looked down on the caribou sleeping undisturbed. Several hunters stationed themselves in each of the four passes out of the valley; then three men walked boldly into the valley spooking the herd, which fled to the nearest pass. There they were met with a deadly volley of fire before they could turn and flee to another pass where they met with the same disastrous result. This happened again and again until the remainder of the herd escaped by sheer weight of numbers through the last pass out of the valley.

Spellbound, I witnessed the slaughter at close hand. The rifle I clutched was forgotten as I stared at the carnage, the terror and the panic in the eyes of the bawling, helpless animals, and the blood spurting from their fatal wounds. I was so shocked and revolted I felt like weeping. Yet I could not feel anger toward those who were inflicting such misery and destruction. This was their living, their traditional pattern of existence in one of the harshest human environments in the world—a cruel necessity for their survival. But for me it was a bitter experience. I knew that from that moment I could never wilfully kill another living creature. My painful and guilty regret was that I learned my lesson in humanity too late to spare the lives of the many beautiful, innocent animals I had destroyed in the ironic name of sport.

Perhaps it was because I was still strongly influenced by my early background while growing up under the guidance of a father whom I greatly admired—a father who was celebrated in our neighborhood, and in fact in the entire state of Tennessee, as a champion with both rod and gun—that at the time I lived in Berea I was not ready to acknowledge any compunction I might tend to feel about killing game animals. And I enjoyed associating with the other hunters in the area with whom I soon became acquainted. All of them had the talent, so common among the Appalachian mountaineers, of being outstanding storytellers, full of colorful anecdotes about their hunting experiences. I also had a fund of hunting stories to share, and the enjoyment of the association seemed to be mutual, though I was sure my talent could never equal theirs.

At first, I found myself somewhat handicapped in my use of language since I thought I could not afford to run the risk of seeming to ridicule my companions by imitating their accents. I tried to avoid using any accents at first, but that hampered my style considerably, and I soon lapsed into quoting the exact idiomatic phrases of the characters in my stories. To my surprise my listeners were greatly amused and actually "cracked up" at the accuracy of my impersonations, and their appreciation of the story itself was obviously intensified. Two of the most admirable characteristics of the mountain people were revealed here—the absence of self-consciousness and the ability to laugh at themselves. I never felt they were simply being courteous when they appeared to thoroughly enjoy my performance.

I had a few stories they seemed never to have heard. I still remember a number of these anecdotes verbatim through having repeated them so often to appreciative listeners, usually other hunters, during the many years up to the present. One of the characteristics of all these shared yarns is that they are seldom true and are not necessarily expected to be by the audience. Naturally, their authenticity is never questioned. New ones are constantly being added to the collection, although they may be introduced as having been dredged up from the past. They include tales of every sort of hunting, such as squirrel hunting, coon hunting, rabbit hunting, even versions of "snipe hunting" (a type of hoax played on strangers and unsuspecting local neophytes in both Appalachia and the outer world). Among the best that I remember are a number about foxhunting—a classic category among these storytellers. To appreciate these stories fully one has to know at least the fundamentals of this sport as it was practiced in the southern mountain regions of the United States. Apparently the only similarity the version practiced in the bluegrass region of Kentucky bears to the traditional English foxhunt is that hounds are employed in the chase.

When I came to Kentucky I had no knowledge of either kind, except what I had heard my father explain about the mountain type, and what I had read in British literature about the English type. I first heard about the English type as it was practiced in the Lexington area from my friends Johnnie and Rena Niles. They were members of the Iroquois Hunt Club, the only one of its kind in the state. On one occasion they had arranged to accompany Jack Tadlock, the kennel man and manager of the stable for the club at that time, on one of his exercise sessions with the hounds. Part of his job was to exercise the pack regularly at night to keep them in top condition for the formal, scheduled hunts with horses during the daytime. Since I expressed great interest in the subject, Rena and Johnnie invited me to go along on one of the night exercise hunts with them and Tadlock. This was a privilege available to any members and guests who might wish to enjoy this extracurricular activity, but apparently there were not a great many who did.

The "informal hunt" was similar to the mountain type foxhunt in two respects—the fox was never caught or killed, and it was always run at night. All that I remember of that experience is that Tadlock met us at the foot of a specified hill and directed us to climb to the crest and wait for him there while he released the pack of hounds from the transport truck. When he rejoined us he led us to a selected spot on the crest from where we could all listen to the chase, which had already begun. This was my first experience at any type of foxhunt, and I must say I found it so enjoyable that I would almost certainly have become an addict of the mountain type hunt, to which I was introduced a little later, if I had ever had the proper environment and opportunity. The pleasure of a few occasional "listeners" to the chase is purely incidental in the English foxhunt, but it is the primary purpose of the mountain type. There is definitely a musical quality in the blending of notes of different pitches in the baying of the hounds. There is also mounting excitement, as the pack dogs close the distance between themselves and the fox, and their baying quickens.

The mountain type of hunt seems to have evolved slowly among the early settlers of the region, where it is now a traditional sport. One surprising aspect of it, as mentioned above, is that the fox is never captured or killed. In fact this is forbidden. This is not through any concern for the animal, per se, but because the hunters want it to survive to be hunted again—the sport requires a handily available quarry.

Each participant in a typical mountain foxhunt has his own hounds, which are part of the pack used by the group of a few enthusiasts in any given area. The hunt may start anytime after dark and the evening meal. The pack—anywhere from five or six to a dozen or more—is taken to an area that foxes are known to inhabit and turned loose. Their owners then climb to a preselected spot to listen to the chase, which begins when one of the hounds hits a fresh scent trail. A campfire is started; the "hunters" simply relax and normally take refreshment from a bottle of moonshine as it is passed around.

A stranger to the sport is inclined to ask, "What's the object?"

The foxhunter would consider this a stupidity. "Why, to hear the purty music of them hounds a-bayin'" would probably be his surprised answer. And this is indeed the sole and dead serious objective, thoroughly enjoyed by the hunters. It is the true attraction to which all mountain foxhunters are addicted and dedicated. But there is another important element involved—it is the rivalry between owners of the hounds. Each owner is very proud of his dogs; he believes his are the best of the pack. The dogs' performance in the hunt arouses intense emotions over the fine points of the sport: whose dog strikes the first scent; how he takes and holds the lead on the trail; how quickly he finds the trail when it has been lost; which hound has the finest "mouth" (that is, voice). All this their masters can determine by ear from their firelit vantage point on a central hilltop where the music of the hounds is clearly audible.

I remember well a story my father told that illustrates the prestige and jealousy that surround the ownership of foxhounds in the mountain communities. He told of talking with a mountain character and of praising one of the man's remote neighbors for his friendliness and helpfulness. The man studied a few moments, then said, "Well, he is, you know—he is a right nice feller in some ways. But he h'aint got ary houn'dog that's wuth a tinker's dam."

One of the best stories concerns a lowlander, a remote relative of one of the mountain foxhunters' wives, who came a-visitin' on one occasion. As a gesture of hospitality the foxhunter invited the man to join him and his neighbors in the usual foxhunt. The visitor had no knowledge whatever of foxhunting, but being somewhat ill at ease in strange company, he went along without asking questions, since his hosts seemed to assume he knew all about the sport.

The group climbed the hill, built their fire, and settled down to listen. Soon the hounds were giving full tongue to the chase. There was rapt silence around the fire until one man gave expression to what they all were thinking. He said to no one in particular, but the stranger thought he was speaking to him, "Now ain't that the purtiest music you ever heered in all yore borned days?"

The stranger listened intently for a few minutes then said, "Well, it might be,—but I cain't hear nothin' fer them damn houn's a-bayin'."

Of course the English type of foxhunt is fundamentally a sport that emphasizes the element of social prestige. Only royalty, the aristocracy, and the socially elite are privileged to enjoy it in Great Britain wherever it is played. In America, the imported version is sometimes looked upon by the unsympathetic as the height of snobbery and is the butt of some hilarious anecdotes. To illustrate, I feel compelled to include here another of my father's stories. It starts with the hackneyed phrase, "it seems."

It seems there was once an overnight American millionaire who had gained his wealth by manufacturing a superior mousetrap. He had always longed to be one of the American "upper crust" as evidenced by membership in an American foxhunt club. But he seriously doubted that he could qualify since he had no practical knowledge of foxhunting procedures and etiquette. However, being an inventor, he finally thought of a way he just might possibly overcome his deficiency. He had been informed by his parents that the family had come to America from England. He hired a genealogist to verify the fact, then applied for membership in an American foxhunt club and was accepted. Of course he would have been accepted without such elaborate preparation simply because of his prodigious wealth, but he was not aware of this. He was an expert horseman due to having spent his youth on a ranch in the West. At least he had no worries there. And he was fortunate enough to locate a retired English valet, who was perfectly qualified to instruct his new master in foxhunt procedure and behavior—in fact, the man proved to be an expert in this field.

Finally the day for the test of the master's newly acquired skill arrived. He and his valet joined one of the club's scheduled hunts and rode all day with the pack of hounds. That evening, after the master's dinner and scotch and soda, he called his valet in to discuss the day's hunt. The following conversation ensued.

The master: "Rare sport we had today, eh what, George?"

George: "Indeed so, sir."

Master: "Well, tell me, George, did you notice me breaking any of the rules about foxhunting you have taught me? I want you to be honest of course if you did."

George: "Well, sir, there was one little thing. Not of any great importance, I'm sure. But I do think it would have been much better to have called out the customary, 'tally-ho! tally-ho!—view hallo' when you sighted the fox, instead of madly yelling, as you did, sir, 'There goes the little son-of-a-bitch!'"

I was honored very early in my residence in Berea by being invited to join the "audience" at one of the local hunts. It was a mark of acceptance, you might say, into a group of somewhat dubious characters in the area. At this point it is time to confess my fascination with these colorful, if slightly disreputable, acquaintances, which led me into some activities during this part of my life in which I can hardly take pride. They were all drinkers, if not drunkards. Most were inveterate gamblers with few morals. As far as I knew, none was a criminal, but some were certainly feudists—or at least from feudist families. I believe it was the language they spoke, the pure vernacular of the first settlers, that first attracted me to an association with this class of citizenry. But I cannot deny enjoying their questionable pastimes as well. I liked sociable drinking; I liked playing pool; I liked playing poker. In the Berea area, no other class of people indulged in these kinds of recreation, at least not openly. Such indulgence was not new to me. Back as far as high school in my native Knoxville, even though I had not acquired a taste for liquor, I had furthered my knowledge of the other two somewhat disreputable pastimes to the point of becoming rather skilled at both. In Berea I soon gained some notoriety as a "shark," and I discovered a pleasant stimulation from moderate drinking. Looking back from the heights of respectable old age, I fully realize how reprehensible my conduct was during that period of my life.

Most regrettable from the practical standpoint was the amount of time that could have been much better spent at perfecting my skill and becoming more prolific as a painter. Still, how differently my career might have developed without such experiences is of course an imponderable question. I have to wonder what life would be like now without the reminiscences that revive those experiences. It cannot be denied that they provided subject matter for some of the paintings I consider to be among my best of that period.

To fully appreciate the social situation in Berea and its standards in the nineteen-thirties and how they affected my behavior, one has to be aware of certain factors that influenced them. Previous to repeal of the prohibition in 1933, the community of Berea had had its own ordinance prohibiting the sale or use of intoxicating beverages within its limits. Beyond these limits the federal statute took over, so that there was no liquor legally available anywhere near the town. With repeal, however, Berea could not prevent establishments selling liquor from taking root on its doorstep, so to speak.

However, the situation became rather complex when national legislation was passed allowing what was called "local option." Under this law, municipalities could pass laws either allowing or prohibiting the use and sale of alcoholic beverages within their limits. Berea remained teetotal of course. Madison County voted to allow beer and wine, while it outlawed hard liquor. But Rockcastle County had no restrictions whatever, except for sales to minors of any type of alcohol, as specified in the national law. Previous to all this new legislation, under the laws of prohibition established by the Eighteenth Amendment and the Volstead Act, drinkers had had to rely on "moonshine," "bathtub gin," "home brew," homemade wine, or other inferior and illegal products. These still existed to some extent, but their use was greatly reduced when common commercial beer and wine became available. Most of the experienced bootleggers of the earlier period became legitimate liquor dealers, as a liquor license was usually not too costly and was easy to obtain in most cases.

One new enterprise was opened up in "the gap," a few miles south of Berea, where U.S. Highway 25 crossed the line between Madison and Rockcastle Counties. This was a strategic location for selling liquor, as it offered the first chance a traveler coming from the north would have to buy any for a good many miles, and it was the last chance for those traveling to the north, out of Rockcastle County and into Madison. Arnold Belcher was the proprietor of the alcoholic enterprise that opened up in this choice location. A well-liked character among the fraternity of amateur gamblers and frequenters of beer joints, liquor stores, and such, his place was so popular that in a remarkably short time a small, scattered community grew up around it. In a few years it became large enough to justify a U.S. post office. Its official name, taken from the sign atop Belcher's place, painted in gargantuan letters, was "LEGAL LIQUOR, KY."

Among the first to take advantage of the change in the law in Madison and Rockcastle Counties was an establishment called, for no known reason, The Manhattan Club. This sprang up just north of the Berea city limits on U.S. Highway 25. It was owned and operated by one of the most personable and colorful characters I have ever known. Clayton Gabbard was a member of the numerous clan of Gabbards inhabiting Madison County. He was also among the most intelligent and attractive of my new acquaintances. Although he spoke the vernacular, on occasion in conversing with outsiders he would reveal his knowledge of somewhat better grammar and usage. For this reason, when we first met I was not aware of his local origin, and it was some time before this became apparent. Unfortunately, I neglected to learn very much about his very early life—he was about thirty when I knew him—but I was able to glean a few facts during our acquaintance.

He had an impressive physique—six feet three or four inches tall by two hundred and thirty pounds—which accounted for his having aspired at one time to become a heavyweight prizefighter. He laughed about this. He had been living in California at the time, where he won a few fights but soon learned he lacked the speed and agility to exist for long as a pro. I believe he ran some sort of business for a while before returning to Kentucky. At any rate, he had a head for business and recognized an opportunity to prosper in running a "beer joint" near a strictly dry community. Besides this, he was a skillful gambler and saw no reason he should not quietly, but profitably, add to his income by this means in his new location.

The Manhattan Club became an almost daily habit with me when taking a break from painting in the studio. I shall make no attempt to claim that one of my assistants aided and abetted in this habit to the point of encouraging it, but Alois Ulrich was an inveterate beer drinker of the old German school, and it was very convenient for us to take our breaks together at the Manhattan. Bert Mullins never joined us; he did not like beer as a beverage, nor did he care for the camaraderie of the other clientele that frequented the club. Alois, I believe, never knew of my other trips "down the hill" in the evenings to indulge my gambling instincts in the basement of the Manhattan. The gatherings there were fairly frequent, involving more or less the same group of a dozen or so gamblers (although never more than seven poker players were in the game at once, of course). I enjoyed these evenings immensely.

It was during the days of my struggle to stay afloat in Chicago that I had fine-tuned my knowledge of poker. I had several friends there, and many evenings were passed at this fascinating game. It may seem odd that during the depression there were people willing to risk money at a game of chance when everyone had so little. But the stakes were always very small in our game, and the players nearly equal in skill, so normally no one won or lost very much. At some early point I got hold of two small paperback books titled *How to Win at Stud Poker* and *How to Win at Draw Poker*, which improved my game tremendously—in fact, to the point that winning became a liability, and I realized I had to rein in my newfound skill or face not being invited to play anymore.

In my new environment there were some very sharp contestants. My skill did not set me apart to any great extent, and I could play with a free hand and not too much advantage. Even so, I found that eventually my winnings mounted to the point that I could afford to buy an almost new second-hand car. I had felt this need keenly ever since coming to Berea. I went often to Lexington, and it was very awkward to have to depend on the bus or some friend who happened to be making the trip in his car. I was now much more mobile and independent. I well remember how exhilarated I was over my improved situation and elevated status as a car owner, something I had never before enjoyed.

I realize this account of my various forms of recreation begins to sound as if I must not have applied myself very diligently to my chosen profession. But I must say, if defensively, that no one other than myself seemed to be aware of this or to criticize me as a time waster. This may have been due to my ability to paint rapidly when at work, and the volume turned out seemed impressive.

(Witness Rannels's comment, quoted earlier, on my completion of the University of Kentucky Library murals.) Still, I could not stifle a feeling of guilt at times over my failure to accomplish more as a painter. I was fully aware that my interests were too scattered—that for full accomplishment one must have a singleness of purpose toward one's work and avoid diversion into exploration of other fields, no matter how intriguing. Still, it is impossible to change one's congenital nature and one's ways of responding to environmental influences, be they favorable or adverse.

Here, I should mention one of the favorable influences fostered by my mother. She began to read to me and my brother from the classics when we were very young. Thus, I grew up with perhaps an unusually early interest in books. My father was as appreciative of literature as my mother. He had been involved with poetry in his early life, having made friends with a fellow Indianian, the "hoosier poet" James Whitcomb Riley. This association led him to try writing verse himself. Unfortunately, he imitated Riley far too successfully; but he soon realized his shortcomings in this field (probably Riley's faults as well) and did not dabble in it for very long.

Rather strangely, I think, although I had this strong early direction of interest in literature, writing was not one of the attractions that seduced me from a straight and narrow path devoted exclusively to painting. However, long before finishing art school, my love of books and reading lead me to realize I should have gone to college first in order to gain a well-rounded, basic education. I began then to be interested in trying to remedy my profound ignorance of so many areas of human thought and knowledge by gaining more understanding of the subjects I was most interested in—art and architecture and their history. Then I was lured on to a study of anthropology, of philosophy via aesthetics, and of psychology. Of course I did not expect to gain much knowledge of any of these subjects on my own and finally accumulated a fundamental grasp of them only by gradual, not very systematic, application to their study over many of my later years.

One of the advantages I found in living and working in Berea was my association with the college and members of its faculty. The college had an excellent library, and it brought many cultural events to the community, such as outstanding musicians and lecturers. It was especially gratifying to have a warm relationship with Mary Ela, the head of the art department, and with members of her staff. Not long before I arrived in Berea, a regeneration of the art department had taken place. It was now housed in a brand-new building on the campus with excellent facilities and equipment, including a small gallery and studios for special classes. Because of the proximity of Lexington, I enjoyed this same kind of pleasant and profitable association with the University of Kentucky, its art department, its teaching personnel, and its students.

My association with the university was, however, at least slightly different from that with the college. The difference lay in the essential difference between the two institutions. The college was primarily a fundamental religious institution, though nonsectarian in its insistence on Christian practice and dogma. All enrolled students were required to take the two-year Bible study course, whatever their major interest. Thus, caution prevented my freely revealing my disbelief in religion if I wished to remain in the good graces of the administration, and indeed those of many of my friends in the community. I have always been careful to follow what I consider some very valuable early advice from my father, who said, "Son, if you have a warm and valued friend you want to keep as such, never discuss either politics or religion with him or her unless you are sure he or she agrees thoroughly with your convictions. Consider tolerance of others' opinions not only a virtue in itself, but a means of self-protection as well."

Although I was thoroughly aware of how important Berea College's program of education for rural Appalachia had become in influencing the lives of young mountain people for the better, I could never accept what I considered its totally illogical and untenable religious beliefs. And I could not stifle a certain impatience with the self-righteous and unreasoning complacency that some members of the faculty and administration so clearly revealed. However, I did not allow these reactions to affect my relationship with others whom I found to embody many of the admirable qualities of true educators.

I knew very well that I was looked upon with some suspicion by at least a few in the college as well as by the conservatives in the town who did not know, but somehow seemed to suspect, my liberal views and attitudes. I believe it was Upton Sinclair who suggested that all artists are suspect in the eyes of the public because they live unconventional lives that allow them lots of time for immoral mischief. The irrepressible Johnnie Niles once said that many of the ultraconservatives of the town would cross themselves twice before going to the other side of the street to pass my studio. What a wag!

CHAPTER 7
Of Easel Paintings and Murals

IT WAS DURING THE FIRST FEW WEEKS of working on the Louisville murals, while the three apprentices were carrying out the preliminary stages, that I was unexpectedly able to spend some time developing what I considered my own "legitimate" kind of work. I was keenly interested in working with the subjects that this new environment offered, both the human subjects and those inspired by nature. In contrast to the "illustrations" of American life that characterized the work sponsored by the Section, I wanted to concentrate on the abstract elements of my subjects, rather than their realistic or sentimental import. I was striving for aesthetic quality, which I considered far more important, and hoping this would be recognized. I really would have preferred to spend all my time and artistic energy in developing a more abstract concept of reality.

In Paris I had been strongly impressed by what I saw and heard discussed of the ideas of a few artists who were striving toward making painting as abstract as the greatest symphonic music, an effect that is purely aesthetic, with no dependence on thematic reference to realistic subject matter. I was unhappy with the Section's influence toward realism, but powerless to alter it, of course.

At this time, I was submitting paintings to some of the principal competitive exhibitions, both local and national, with some degree of success. In response to the resultant publicity, I was invited to speak to several groups in Lexington and Louisville interested in the arts. All of this helped my work to become better known, which as every artist knows, is necessary if his career is to prosper. I was invited to have a one-man show at the J. B. Speed Museum in Louisville and was accepted in two national shows in New York. (Unfortunately, after so many years I no longer have clippings or correspondence to document my activities of that period. This makes the dates I venture to give uncertain at best.)

I was always surprised at the amount of interest my work appeared to generate. One instance was when Sadakichi Hartmann, the well-known artist, writer, and art critic, selected me along with some dozen or so other American artists as those most likely to have a lasting influence on the art of this country. I was still more astonished when he later shrank the list to ten and still kept my name on it. I had no idea how he could have become acquainted enough with my work to make that appraisal. I understand that in a book published shortly after this he tried to explain his dubious choices. My financial condition at the time did not allow me to squander its modest price, and I have never seen the book and cannot now remember its title.

This complete lack of cash, though momentary, was a very common situation to be faced during that period, not only by me but by many other artists working on commission for the Section of Fine Arts. The periodic installments—on signing the contract for the work, when the work was judged half-finished, on completion, and at final approval—were often very slow in coming. Although I felt my career was advancing satisfactorily as far as recognition was concerned, without the mural contracts it offered very poor financial returns. The occasional sales of paintings were few and far between, and the prices for works by a relatively unknown artist were very modest at best. Even so, I was not completely dissatisfied. All I wanted was to be able to continue painting. I felt very strongly that an artist's only justifiable ambition is to attain the perfection of his or her art—gaining fame or fortune should never be the ultimate goal.

It was sometime while we were working on the Louisville murals that I entered a Section of Fine Arts competition for the Jackson, Mississippi, federal courthouse and post office. I believe this competition was regional in scope, confined to artists from a group of southern states including Kentucky. I entered because I realized that I would have to try for any available project I might qualify for if I hoped to continue to survive the depression, regardless of my interest, or lack of it, in the work itself.

To prepare for submitting a design in this instance, I made a trip to Jackson. I had never been in the state of Mississippi before. I was unacquainted with its people, its topography, or much of anything else about it that might have excited my interest. I was not at all in favor of trying to paint historical subjects, believing that this always results in distortion, since it is impossible for an artist to render the effect accurately of an event he has not experienced himself. I knew I could not gain any helpful impression of the state by the trip; I only felt it necessary to see the space in the courtroom designated for the mural. I believed this could stimulate a design that would be in harmony with both the architecture and the purpose of the room. It had seemed from the start that I would have to choose some aspect of the judicial process, in keeping with the location that had been chosen for the mural.

My imperfect memory of the design I came up with sees a giant, illusionary, robed figure of a judge almost filling the upper half of the wall space behind and above the judge's bench. The figure is brooding over a mélange of figures and scenes below, representing various features of the judicial and law enforcement branches of the system represented by the court. In spite of all my efforts, I had little confidence that this concept could win the contest. I considered the idea trite, at best. I felt its only merit was in the design looked at as a harmonious abstraction, pleasing to the eye and the viewer's sense of form, space, and color. Other than that, I felt it was undistinguished and not representative of my best capabilities. I was not at all surprised when it was rejected. I was well-nigh astonished when it was selected as one of the three best designs submitted and learned that the artists of all three of those designs were to be awarded contracts for murals in other locations that the Section felt the artists were capable of executing. Because no design won the Jackson competition, that project was canceled.

I was offered a commission for three rather large panels in the lobby of the Hagerstown, Maryland, post office. This eastern area of the country was also one with which I was almost completely unacquainted. Again, I had to select a subject not specifically related to the location, but that had some more or less universal interest. I decided on some aspects of the postal service. This was, of course, a fairly popular subject among competitors for post office murals. In researching the subject and how to deal with it I hoped to find some aspect that had not been "done to death." I came up with the idea of depicting the interior of a mail car, showing what goes on while the crew is preparing for the mail run to the cities on the route. I chose

Waiting for the Mail, *photo after installation in the Hagerstown, Maryland, post office, 1938. Courtesy National Archives.*

Unloading the Mail, *photo after installation in the Hagerstown, Maryland, post office, 1938. Courtesy National Archives.*

Sorting the Mail, *photo after installation in the Hagerstown, Maryland, post office, 1938. Courtesy National Archives.*

this subject for the central, largest panel of the three—approximately eight by fifteen feet. For the two other panels, somewhat shorter in width, I elected to show mail delivery in a city and the unloading of mail from a mail car in a rail terminal. The figures in all of these designs were life-size in scale.

Fortunately, the date set for the completion of this contract was very liberal, and I did not feel under any pressure to produce and submit the designs while completing my work on the Louisville murals. That time-consuming project was nearly finished, and I had submitted photographs of it to the section, before I felt compelled to begin the research into my ideas for the Hagerstown panels.

I went first to the postal service office in Cincinnati, Ohio, where I obtained permission to visit a mail car while the crew was working against the clock in preparing for the day's run. I worked on pencil sketches from one extreme end of the car where I was out of the way. Working as unobtrusively as possible, I seemed almost unnoticed by the personnel.

Back in the studio, I planned the composition of this scene to show as much detail of the activities of the crew as possible. This involved taking some liberties with the perspective. If photographic technology had included the development of the wide-angle lens at that point in its history, I would certainly have utilized this device, but it came on the market just a bit later. The wide-angle perspective was exactly what was needed to spread out the interior so that the view could show all the clerks at work—normal perspective could not have handled the problem. I made the adjustment in my sketch, trusting that most viewers of the finished murals would understand the liberty I took with reality to show a complete representation of what goes on in a mail car. Still I remember well the indignation of a former postal worker who was upset that I made the interior of the car look like a "parlor." He wrote that he would like to catch me stooping over, rump to the rear, like one of the workers I showed in the mural in perfect position for a swift kick! This criticism seems not to have been shared by the Section, which gave its approval to the sketches that I submitted. These sketches, of course, were followed closely in the preparation of the mural itself.

The Section was not slow in approving the photographs I sent of the finished murals for Louisville. Bert went to work immediately and shipped the ten canvases, removed from the stretcher frames, to the post office in the Louisville Federal Building. Two "technicians" were sent from Washington by the Section to mount them in place. They were obviously experienced in this procedure. I believe they were personnel of the Bureau of Standards. My other two assistants had returned to Louisville, their jobs terminated when the paintings were finished, but Bert and I gave what assistance we could in the installation process. The first step was to coat the mural spaces with a special adhesive formulated in the Bureau of Standards laboratory. It was a compound originated by an Alexander Abels, the head, I believe, of the department concerned with paints and varnishes. He was purported to be a "paint chemist." The material was very difficult to apply because of its viscosity and a resistance to spreading evenly. All the installation I had done previously was with the traditional white lead paste. However, Bert and I were not asked to do any of the application of the adhesive. My memory is that it required the better part of two days to complete the installation of the ten panels.

I was somewhat disappointed that there had been no provision for mounting plaques under the panels giving the date, the title of each, and, of course, the name of the artist. I was gratified when, in a revival of interest in the murals of the depression period, this was finally taken care of in 1989 after the murals were cleaned and restored for the first time. A significant complication connected with the installation occurred a few weeks later when one of the canvases came loose from the wall and had to be reinstalled. This was not the only problem I would have with the Section's adhesive.

Of course I was pleased when the Louisville murals received very favorable publicity in several of the state's newspapers and I began to be called Kentucky's foremost artist. I had gained some distinction during these years of the early thirties from my works that were shown in national exhibitions, but these murals could be viewed by the citizens as having been created specifically for their city and for their gratification. Of course this meant nothing as far as certification of the works' artistic merit was concerned; but I enjoyed the publicity because it helped my professional reputation considerably.

I could now turn my complete attention to the murals for Hagerstown. I had to work without Bert's help, as his WPA status had ended along with that of the other two assistants. He was now devoting his time fully to his own painting and to the monumental task of building his home and studio on Clear Creek. It was not long before he also gave up his part of the studio we had been sharing. This meant that I would have to find other help when I needed assistance with building frames, stretching canvases, and other tasks.

It was at this point that I became acquainted with Alonzo Durham. I can't recall the circumstances of our meeting, but I think it was more than likely at the Manhattan Club, probably over a beer. Alonzo had the misfortune of having become somewhat of an outcast because of his status as an ex-convict. When I met him, he had just been released on parole from the state penitentiary when that institution was inundated during the Ohio River flood of 1937. The water covered a large area, including parts of Louisville. It flooded basements and underground storage areas in that city, including the basement of the J. B. Speed Museum just after an exhibition closed there that included my portrait of John Jacob Niles. The painting floated for several days in the museum basement, I was told, until finally rescued. It ultimately came back to me, and I was able to restore it, restretching the canvas (as I remember it) over a particle board backing, then restoring its surface to its original condition. When I examined the painting recently, it appeared to have survived this drastic experience admirably. Only the wooden stretcher frame was warped, which is what had made the remounting on the solid backing necessary.

This portrait had been painted not long after I met Johnnie Niles. I had made a sketch of him as he played and sang in my studio, and I painted the portrait later without his knowledge. As always, in my paintings of people I did not strive for a photographic image. Painting from memory and my small sketch, I revealed the singer with his mouth open and his head thrown back in his characteristic full-throated singing attitude, his hands keying the strings of the dulcimer as it rested on his knees. It was a very successful effort to show the artist at the emotional peak of his performance. At one of the big shows in New York it attracted attention. *Time* magazine reported, "Frank Long painted John Jacob Niles with his 'dulcinet.'" This was an egregious mistake, one such as is not often made by *Time*, and one that reveals how little is known generally about the dulcimer. Of course, there is no such thing as a "dulcinet," musically or otherwise.

At a later date, the Nileses commissioned Victor Hammer, a Viennese artist who had come to Lexington to teach at Transylvania University, to paint a portrait of Johnnie. He was of the European realist school, and the painting he did was an excellent slick, photographic likeness of the singer. When it was shown to me, I had to bite my tongue to refrain from asking, "Where's the Lord Calvert." (At that time the company that marketed that brand of whiskey was running a series of ads in national magazines called "Men of Distinction," each featuring a tycoon of the business world with a glass of Lord Calvert in his hand.) Although Johnnie and Rena seemed to think very highly of the work, to me it seemed to embody the very worst features of Johnnie's personality—his unbridled vanity and egotism. It suggested nothing of his quality as a great musician.

I remember well that I had just completed my picture of Johnnie when a portraitist from New York came to Berea to do a portrait of the college president, Dr. William J. Hutchins. One of the college's many donors had funded the commission for the artist, a well-known New York portrait painter named Miller. I was surprised when he came one morning to my studio saying he had heard of me and wanted to meet me. My painting was on my easel when he came in. He gazed at it for a long moment, then said, "Well, that's a new wrinkle." I took that to be something of a compliment, intended or not.

Miller (I never learned his full name) was a professional portrait painter, academic and realistic, who painted portraits that were expected by the patrons to be accurate likenesses in a photographic sense. Hutchins sat for him several times, I was told, until the work was finished. But the portrait was never shown publicly (or at least I never saw it), although I understand the artist was paid for his efforts. Apparently, Hutchins was not at all pleased with it. He is said to have called it "an excellent portrait of a suit of clothes."

Bert Mullins became acquainted with the artist, and apparently their friendship blossomed while Miller was in Berea. Later that summer, Bert and Eva visited Miller at his summer place, on Cape Cod, I believe, where they remained for a considerable period. In Bert's biographical sketch in *Who's Who in American Art*, Miller is listed as his teacher. (Incidentally, there is no mention of Bert's study or association with me in any capacity.)

But let me return to Alonzo and why he had been incarcerated at the state's expense. I had heard the story before, and it was much the same when he told it to me soon after our first acquaintance. I believe he was about twenty when he and two others near the same age decided to rob the Boone Tavern. Alonzo made no excuses for this rash act. It seemed it was "Poozy" Cruze, the apparent leader of the trio, who had this brilliant idea to improve what they considered their unsatisfactory financial condition. They entered the hotel after midnight when only the night clerk was on duty. At gunpoint, they took what cash was on hand (I never heard how much) and started driving north on the main highway out of town. The night clerk immediately called the local police, who called the police in Richmond, fifteen miles away, who called the state highway patrol, who set up a roadblock and arrested the trio without any resistance.

After hearing this story from Alonzo I was somewhat puzzled. One might well conclude from the evidence that the participants in this farcical episode were mentally defective, yet I somehow had an illogical feeling that Alonzo was not a criminal type and that he had more intelligence than the facts indicated. For one thing, he spoke better English than his associates, having graduated from the local high school. On my invitation Alonzo appeared one morning at my studio door. He was apparently astonished at the fact that I was an artist, making a living painting pictures. Of course I was sure that astonishment was the prevalent feeling of more than half the Berea population, but with Alonzo there seemed to be an enormous amount of respect attached to this attitude. Possibly this influenced me in his favor, but at any rate, I had an unexplainable feeling that he was worth more than was indicated by the episode of the robbery. I naturally felt some compassion for him in his difficult situation, as well as curiosity about both his intelligence and his character. I remember thinking that even if he didn't have any common sense, he perhaps had some other kind. So I hired him to assist me with the purely manual concerns of the Hagerstown job. He was an adequately handy helper in building the stretcher frames, stretching and preparing the canvases, running errands, and keeping the studio tidy. He was well built and reasonably interesting in appearance, so I found it sometimes appropriate to use him as a model for some of the figures in the murals. I had not used models in any of the others, and indeed it was not necessary here; but it was fun to see the likeness of Alonzo develop as the central figure swinging a full mailbag in the center panel. He seemed a type one might expect to find as a mail car employee.

In the beginning the Section of Fine Arts had no written standards regarding technical requirements to be followed by artists who won commissions in their competitions. But before I began the Hagerstown murals I was notified that I must submit a list of the materials and techniques I planned to use in executing them. The Section's approval was supposed to assure the permanence of the finished work.

It happened that I had concentrated from the start of my career on sound craftsmanship. I studied paint chemistry, the manufacture of artists' colors and materials, and how these should be applied. I was given to understand that only artists' colors that had been tested by the Bureau of Standards would be approved. Under the new regulation, which had not been in effect on the Louisville commission, this meant that the colors of my own manufacture would now be excluded. The Bureau could hardly be expected to go to the considerable expense of testing these for the work of just one artist. I understood this.

However, when I proposed to use colors manufactured by the Permanent Pigments Company of Cincinnati, this was refused. I had used these to some extent on the Louisville job when I began to exhaust the supply of my own colors. Although at that time I would have like to have produced an adequate supply of these, I felt I did not have the considerable amount of time to spare that this would have required. Before using the Permanent Pigments I had made a trip to Cincinnati, where I was given a complete tour of the plant by the management. They answered all my questions to my satisfaction, even allowing me to watch the various processes from start to finish. With this highly satisfactory experience in mind, I naturally wanted to know why the Section refused to sanction these materials in which I had complete confidence.

This was one of the reasons I decided to make a trip to Washington. I also wanted to discuss certain aspects of the Hagerstown job. But I was even more anxious to meet and talk with Ed Rowan and other members of the Section's personnel. I had an idea it might be an advantage in the future to know them a little more intimately.

In thinking about the trip, I concluded it would be a good idea to take Alonzo with me. It would make the trip both less tiring and less tiresome, and of course it is always safer for two to travel together by auto in case of accident. I knew he would be most enthusiastic about the trip. He was an ardent baseball fan, having played the game in high school, and this was June, almost the height of the season. I was sure he would jump at the chance to see the Washington Senators play. I was not at all interested in baseball, having played only football and run track in school, but somehow I felt that Alonzo deserved to be indulged; he had been working faithfully at any task I had given him. Too, I felt a kind of sympathy for him that I could not quite explain, other than natural sympathy for the underdog. It was a two-day trip of more than six hundred miles through some of the most beautiful country in eastern America—the Appalachian mountains and their foothills in West Virginia and Virginia. I had been only as far as Charleston, West Virginia, before, so the second half of the journey was new to me. I think Alonzo enjoyed the scenery almost as much as I did, although he didn't talk about it.

In Washington we had no trouble locating the Section of Fine Arts in the Department of the Interior building, where I was directed to Rowan's office. As Edward Bruce's assistant, Rowan was in charge of the competitions for mural commissions. My correspondence had been almost exclusively with him, the latest of course having been concerning the Hagerstown commission. He was a comparatively young man, and I had never seen any list of his accomplishments or any statement of his qualifications for his job. He had always been affable and had praised my work on the Louisville murals as well as some of my designs for other competitions. However, I had been somewhat discouraged over the handling of the Jackson, Mississippi, competition, although I didn't know for sure whom to blame.

When I brought up the question of why the Permanent Pigments colors were not approved, he took me to see the head of the department that had jurisdiction in the Bureau of Standards. This was Alexander Abels, who turned out to be a chemist of German extraction with a rather forbidding countenance. In answer to the same question he said, "Vell, Mr. Long, ze Bermanent Bigments' gadmiums iss prezibidated und nod zolid. Zo I gannot bermit zeir bigments being used."

I was astonished at this statement and showed it when I replied, "Mr. Abels, according to my study of color manufacture that makes no sense. Although there may be some variation of methods, in all the processes of obtaining cadmium as a pigment, precipitation is involved."

I went on to describe the process, but he—obviously surprised and shocked—interrupted me by blurting out, "Oh vell! zome says dat, bud id iss not zo" and simply walked hastily away, terminating any discussion before it started.

I found out later that the only colors he would sanction were of German manufacture—either Schmincke or Rembrandt. I do not know if their use meant anything to Abels financially, but to me it seemed very suspicious. Those colors are no doubt soundly permanent, but at that time, being imported, they cost almost double the price of the Permanent Pigments. I considered discussing my concerns further with Rowan, but decided not to, being sure this would lead nowhere. I had to explore other possibilities if I could find any. I could not believe Abels was as ignorant of his profession as this incident would indicate. It seemed to me he must have used that random excuse for his negation against Permanent Pigments just to put off someone he thought would be ignorant enough of paint manufacture to accept it. The experience was somewhat unsettling.

Back in Rowan's office I was introduced to Edward Bruce and other members of his staff. Bruce impressed me with his sincerity and his ability to rationalize his artistic philosophy. But I had not been impressed by the few examples of his painting I had seen. Above all, I was alienated by his obvious contempt for the French modernists who were discovering new ways of looking at the world and creating what they saw. As I have stated before, I was not at all in sympathy with his dream of creating an American school of painting by concentrating the murals program on the development of regional realism.

That afternoon we went to the ball game. Alonzo, usually not very demonstrative, showed an enthusiasm he could not suppress. Of course I cannot remember any details of the game, including whom the Senators were playing, or who won. I believe I must have taken a nap during its progress. If Alonzo was disgusted with me he suppressed any impulse he may have had to show it. We took in a movie that evening and left for home early the next morning.

Back in Berea, I happened to get into conversation one morning with Edward Lacey in the Porter-Moore Drug Store. He was one of the two practicing lawyers in town. He was well known in Richmond, the Madison County seat, where he frequently represented clients in county court cases. He also sold insurance. I never knew his origin, but in spite of some superficial refinements, he was obviously from eastern Kentucky. He had the unmistakable nasal twang, as well as the colorful, eccentric speech of the native mountain people. I always enjoyed talking with him to further acquaint myself with variations in the vernacular. He was obviously anxious to make a name for himself as well as a fortune from his professional abilities. His ostentatious flourishing of a big diamond ring and driving of an expensive car were amusing clues to his personality.

It was always entertaining to get Frankie Kinnard, one of the town's most interesting and celebrated personalities, about whom I will have more to say shortly, started on his rabid excoriation of Lacey, whose ostentation and frequent misuse of the English language often goaded Frankie into a frenzy of ridicule. Lacey's sign in the window of his west-end office was a major target. It read *Edward Lacey, Attorney-At-Law, Insurance Agent—A Policy for Ever Need.* If someone mentioned Lacey's name to Frankie he would snort, "Oh! You mean 'A policy for Ever Need' I suppose. If you question this usage that ignoramus will argue it is proper English. What kind of a lawyer is that?"

Actually, Lacey's speech was a small cut above that habitually in use by most native members of the community; he had had a better education than most, and some of it had stuck. He avoided many of the local faults of grammar, and by that accomplishment he assumed he was speaking "good English."

Anyway, during our conversation that morning I told Edward about my problem with the Section over my wish to use the Permanent Pigments. I asked if, since they were unauthorized, I could get into trouble legally if I dared to use them surreptitiously anyway. He studied for a minute or two, then responded, "You say you're shore them colors won't fade or crack later on—that is in a matter of a good many year do you?"

"Yes, I'm sure of that."

"Well," he said, "you don't think they're a-gonna send some guy a-gumshoein' around to yore studio at night and a-testin' them colors to see what yo're a-usin' do you?"

I had to admit I didn't, and we both laughed.

"Well," he said, "I shore think hit's worth the chance and go ahead an' use 'em."

I thought this made good sense; it was what I had decided before I asked, but I found it reassuring to have some "expert" advice to support my decision. Lacey went on to say he was certain the government would not consider any penalty for my not following its rules in this instance, even if someone should discover it, unless there were some obvious failure in the permanence of the murals painted with them.

Suddenly he said, "Now wait a minute! Did you sign anything a swearin' to foller them regalations about the colors? No? Then you don't have nothin' to worry about." So I went merrily on with no qualms in ignoring the Section's unwarranted restriction.

I remember that I was able to spend a considerable amount of time reading while working on the Hagerstown murals. Berea College had an excellent library, and I enjoyed talking to the professors as well. My friend the doctor, Alson Baker, was also well educated and quite well read. We had many discussions of the works of various authors. He was surprisingly capable of enjoying James Joyce's *Ulysses*, which I had come to consider the greatest masterpiece of modern English prose. We had conversations too about the nineteenth-century British poets and the French Symbolists and Decadents. But probably the subject of greatest mutual interest was Thomas Wolfe's works. We had been overwhelmed by *Look Homeward, Angel*. It came closer to portraying our own backgrounds than any other book we had ever encountered.

And there was no lack of opportunities to discuss art. The art department of the college, under the capable direction of Mary Ela, was a continuous source of interest, and a place to indulge in discussions of what was going on in the art world, especially in the American scene. I believe she understood and sympathized with my dissatisfaction in having to spend most of my time concentrating on mural painting, in which I was not wholeheartedly interested. She was also greatly interested in the easel paintings I was creating in my efforts to develop a personal style leaning toward the abstract. I found these discussions with her helpful in clarifying my thinking about what I hoped to achieve in my work, apart from the murals.

CHAPTER 8
A Turkey Shoot with Jessie Kinnard

I REMEMBER IT WAS DURING WORK on the Hagerstown project that I participated in one of the favorite recreations of the local male population on holidays—a turkey shoot. Although this was not my first experience with this indigenous American sport, it was my first turkey shoot in the Berea area, and one of the highlights of the process of my assimilation into the Berea population.

It served also as my first acquaintance with one of the most interesting of the local characters—the well-known Jessie Kinnard. He was the brother of Frankie Kinnard, whom I had previously had the pleasure of meeting. Both brothers were original eccentrics who helped to enliven the Berea scene, but eccentricity seemed almost their only feature in common. They were actually almost as different as the proverbial night and day. Of course they had a few similarities, but they were fundamentally antagonistic types.

Jessie was a pillar, though somewhat warped, of the community, and particularly of the Methodist church. In appearance he attracted attention, being medium tall and carrying his spare frame very erectly except for his head, which was tilted at an odd angle upward and to the left. This, I learned in time, was caused by the fact that he had only one good eye, the one on the right having been replaced with a glass substitute. He was in his early sixties when I knew him, but he appeared to me to be younger, mainly I think because of his very positive and energetic manner.

It was very early on Thanksgiving morning in 1934 that I was startled awake in my studio quarters by a vigorous pounding on the door into the hall from the part I used as a bedroom. Opening the door sleepily, and in my pajamas, I found myself facing the man just described. He grimaced with what would pass for a smile while sticking out his hand and almost shouting, "Are you Mr. Long?—are you Mr. Long?" (I soon learned he had a habit of repeating his first words of any introductory sentence.)

At my acknowledgment of the name, he went on, "Well, I'm Jessie Kinnard, Jessie Kinnard, and I'll tell you why I have come to see you, Mr. Long. They're a-havin' a turkey shoot down at Renfro Valley and I want to take you down there and get you to win me a turkey. I've got my son, Junior, to drive us in my brand new Buick—he's a good driver, so get your clothes on and let's go!"

I was overwhelmed by the sheer audacity of the man and astonished at this presumptuous invitation, which seemed to be a peremptory command. Why had he picked me for this particular honor?

Apparently he could read my thoughts, as he went on after a moment, "Of course I know you're a damn good shot, or I wouldn't be here a-askin' you. Of course I'll pay fer the shots, and I've got three good twenty-twos in the car fer you to take yer pick, unless you've got one of your own you want to shoot."

At this point I had regained some of my poise and decided I would go along with this absurd proposal just to find out more about the decidedly strange old coot who made it. I protested that I was not really an exceptional offhand marksman and asked where he had heard I was.

With obvious annoyance, he said, "Aw come on! Mr. Long. There's no virtue in modesty. Why I know all about you. Do you think I'd be stupid enough to want you to shoot fer me if I didn't?"

I decided I would let him know I wasn't so flattered I had lost sight of my own interests, so I said, "Tell me, Mr. Kinnard, just what's in this for me?"

He seemed outraged. "Why, I'm a-offerin' you free transportation—and I know you like to shoot. I know you don't have a car of your own, so I thought you'd jump at the chance to enjoy a turkey shoot at no cost to yourself. What more do you want?"

After a moment of silence while I waited he said, "I'll tell what I'll do. I'll pay fer the shots fer yer own turkey up to one dollar—ten shots." I had heard that this was a fairly common agreement between good shots and their sponsors. So I agreed. I had no use for a turkey—I was invited out to dinner that night and I knew no one who might not have a turkey already in the oven—but I was intrigued by the situation and the character of the man. I got dressed while he and his eighteen-year-old son waited in the car, and we took off at rather excessive speed. At my request we stopped at the west end of town at the Sunset Inn restaurant. This was operated by the now famous Colonel Sanders of the fried chicken business. Sanders had come to Berea from Middlesboro, I believe, and returned there not long after, not having prospered in Berea.

While the Kinnards waited in the car, I had breakfast. Shortly after we took off again, Jessie Kinnard began to cross-examine me intensively. He was an expert who could easily have succeeded, without any special training, as a criminal trial lawyer. He soon knew where I came from, what I did for a living, how I happened to come to Berea, and other details of my life too numerous to mention. Among his questions, he asked if I knew his brother, Frankie.

When I said I did he asked, "Well what do you think of him?"

"Why, I like Frankie very much," I replied. "He's one of the most interesting characters I've met in Berea."

"Is that so?" he asked, as if surprised. "Black sheep of the family," he said with a snort, then asked, "How do you think he gets along?"

"What do you mean?"

"Well, did you ever see him a-workin' at anything? No? Well, how do you think he makes a livin'?"

"I have no idea," I said. "It never occurred to me to wonder."

With mounting impatience he almost shouted, "Well, how do you think he manages to eat, pay his bills, have a place to sleep and clothes to wear?"

When I failed to reply he paused; then with a curl of his lip and a wry smile he said, "Well *I* keep him up—*I pay his bills!*"

I had heard that Frankie was epileptic, so it was no surprise that someone was providing his living, but I was surprised his brother was doing it with so little grace or charity. Later, when I learned more about these two, this became understandable, though hardly excusable.

They were important characters in the verbal archives of Berea, so attentively maintained by all who delighted in sharing their flavorful humor. There were a dozen stories or more, with others appearing at irregular intervals, all centering on the brothers' eccentricities, their mental and physical abnormalities, or the radical differences in their respective characters and temperaments.

I especially liked the story about their having taken a trip together a good many years before, when Jessie was employed as a traveling agent for a line of cosmetics sold to drugstores and beauty parlors. No one seemed to know why Frankie went along on this occasion, but Jessie must have had a good reason. On the very first day of the trip, Frankie managed to escape his brother's close surveillance long enough to get gloriously drunk. That night Jessie, as usual, removed his glass eye and placed it in a glass of water by their bed. Frankie awoke with raging thirst due to his excessive alcoholic consumption and drank the water, including Jessie's glass eye, on which he strangled. Jessie, rather than lose the glass eye (not for any concern for Frankie), beat his brother on the back until Frankie disgorged the eye. In telling the story, Jessie would add with vindictive malice, ignoring the obvious fallacy of his conclusion, "and if I hadn't been there, the little son-of-a-bitch would have choked to death."

Frankie would gleefully tell his version of the incident. He delighted in revealing Jessie's stupid error in his conclusion that if he had not been present his brother would have choked to death. But he would never do this in his brother's presence. He knew this would spoil the joke, which depended for its most telling effect on Jessie remaining ignorant of how thoroughly he was being made a fool of.

Besides being a supporter of the community Jessie was also a deacon of the Methodist church. He was one of the deacons who sat on the front row every Sunday to listen to the sermon. He habitually assumed a rather grotesque position, his left arm extended along the back of the pew, and his left leg extended fully on the seat, which terminated at the aisle. In this position he could view the rest of the congregation with his one good eye by only half turning his head. He could thus take note of which members attended church and which were backsliders. While engaged in his scrutiny of the congregation he would often remove his glass eye and spend the time cleaning and polishing it with his silk handkerchief reserved for Sundays. The preacher was not too pleased with this distracting performance, but since Jessie was a major contributor to the church fund, he had to suffer in silence along with other members of the congregation who found this performance highly distasteful if not revolting.

Both Kinnard brothers had had a relatively good education, to which they responded quite differently. Frankie was well read and had an appreciation of literature and the arts. Jessie was of a more practical nature. Frankie spoke reasonably correct English, while Jessie often lapsed into the ungrammatical idiom of the vernacular, although he knew better. He was the older of the two and had raised a family.

Henry, his older boy, now in his thirties, had not been successful at anything he had tried and of course was a disappointment to Jessie. The younger son, Junior, our present chauffeur, was a typical teenager of the times with little respect for his family. One of the stories in the Kinnard saga told how Junior would take the opportunity, when his father was in the bathroom, to lock him in and refuse to release him until he slipped a ransom of folding money under the door.

It seems that almost the only characteristic Jessie and Frankie had in common was a quirky sense of humor. Bessie Gay, the wife of a local farmer whom I got to know years after coming to Berea, told of speaking to Jessie one morning as she was going up the post office steps while Jessie was going down. They had the following brief conversation:

She—"Good morning, Mr. Kinnard."

He—"Well hello! Do you know me?"

She—"Why, of course, Mr. Kinnard. Everybody knows you."

He—"They do? Well, what do they think of me?"

She—"Why they think you're a fine man, Mr. Kinnard."

He—"Well, that ain't the way they treat me. By the way, do you know my son Henry?"

She—"Yes, I do."

He—"Well, well! And did you ever sleep with him?"

She—indignantly—"Why, of course not!"

He—roaring with laughter—"Then you don't know my son Henry!"

Bessie was insulted, but the story was funny and she liked to tell it.

I was fortunate in being at the scene when another fabulous story was added to the fund of those about the Kinnards. It happened at Keeneland, the bluegrass racetrack near Lexington. In spite of his hard-nosed religious belief, Jessie had several irreligious habits such as glib profanity and betting on the horses. On this occasion I happened to be included in a party of a few friends of the Kinnards who were invited to accompany them on the outing. Junior, as usual, was the designated driver of our car, and also as usual, he paid no attention whatever to his father's directions and criticisms. He broke the speed limit consistently against Jessie's blasphemous commands to slow down.

From time to time Jessie would crane his neck across Junior's lap to see the speedometer. He would then look at his watch and write something in the little notebook he carried. After a short interval he would again go through the same maneuver. Then, with astonishing inconsistency, he would proudly announce, "Well, we made the last five miles on this twisty road in under four minutes. That's pretty good, that's pretty good, ain't it?"

In his indulgence in the sport of kings Jessie was a firm believer in the "scientific" study of the racing forms to select the horses he backed. Frankie, on the other hand, was sure his study of the *appearance* of the horses in the paddock, coupled with his intuition, was far to be preferred. Of course he had no money of his own to invest, but in spite of no success he would try diligently to influence Jessie. In one high-stakes race Frankie was especially sure that he had picked the winner. This was a horse named Menow, and Frankie was particularly insistent in his recommendations to Jessie.

He said, "Jessie, for God's sake bet on this horse. I know he is gonna win, I feel it in my bones, and I have *never* been wrong when I had this feeling." He was practically in tears, but Jessie, as usual, brushed him off as if he was nothing but a pest. He had already made his "scientific" choice. As luck would have it, Menow *was* the winner at high odds, and Frankie, in a rage, confronted Jessie.

"Why, you bastard!" he shouted at the top of his voice. "I told you Menow was gonna win and you wouldn't listen, you old bastard!"

This drew Jessie's wrath, and he shouted back for all the world to hear, "Why you little son-of-a-bitch, don't you *ever* call your brother a bastard. That's an insult to our mother."

Of course Jessie had much to legitimately complain about in his brother's behavior. He had tried to set Frankie up in a business he could manage in spite of his affliction. He chose the chicken business and had an elaborate chicken farm laid out and constructed in an open area on the land adjoining the property where he had built a small, four-room house for Frankie to occupy. He chose white leghorn chickens as good layers for the eggs and for their highly palatable flesh. Unfortunately, before the business could get going, Frankie felt he must celebrate. He invited his dissolute friends to a party that lasted more than a week, night and day, during which time the fifty chickens of the starting stock were consumed as sustenance for the indefatigable poker players, crap shooters, and moonshine liquor guzzlers. Apparently, Frankie felt no qualms over the fiasco. Jessie had not consulted him, and he didn't want to be in the chicken business anyhow. Of course I had not heard all these anecdotes about the Kinnards at the time of the trip to the turkey shoot. I was not prepared for Jessie's eccentricities. I was only aware that I was traveling with a very unpredictable character whom I would do well to watch.

Our trip was short, and I was somewhat relieved when Jessie left off his catechizing as we came in sight of a cluster of buildings ahead. These consisted of a few dwellings and a filling station, the first outpost of the community of Renfro Valley, which is only a few miles south of Berea on U.S. Highway 25. It was really quite small, hardly even a town at this time. As he sighted the gas station Jessie told Junior to pull over for instructions. As we drove up, a sleepy-looking attendant appeared and Jessie called out to him, "Hey there, we're a-lookin' fer the turkey shoot. Where's it at?"

"Why I don't rightly know whur it's at, mister."

"Well hell, man, this is Renfro Valley ain't it? *This* is where they're a-havin' it."

"Well, I think I did hear some shots a while ago. I think they was a-comin' from down thar around the next bend in the road. I s'pose that might be the turkey shoot."

This seemed to infuriate Jessie. He fairly shouted, "You *think!* you *suppose!* do you? The fact is you ain't got sense enough to know your ass from a hole in the ground. Drive on, Junior, dammit, drive on."

I was somewhat alarmed at this outburst. In this area such abusive talk could get a man killed. But I guess Jessie had analyzed the nature of his victim and knew he was in no danger. The man just stared at him as if puzzled.

Sure enough, as we rounded the next bend in the road, near the center of a level meadow there was a gathering of perhaps a dozen or more men with guns in hand. There was also another group of about as many men and boys who were possibly mere spectators—or innocent bystanders, if you will. Jessie had seen to it that we would get an early start, and it seemed clear that the activity was in its very first stage. From the road we could view the whole layout. Several other cars and trucks were parked not far from the firing line. Some were occupied by women and young children who were apparently there just to watch the "goin's on" in relative comfort. Nearby were two trucks parked together at the far end of the firing line. One had several cases of soft drinks in tubs of cracked ice; the other held some crates containing live chickens and turkeys.

We pulled off the road and parked near the other cars. Jessie started immediately toward a man standing near the trucks with the live targets and motioned me to come along. He introduced me to Henry O'Dell, the operator of this enterprise, by proclaiming, "Henry, this here is Mr. Frank Long—Mr. Frank Long. He's gonna shoot fer me today an' I'm a-bettin' he'll win me a turkey." He grinned as he said it, and Henry laughed as we shook hands and replied, "Well, I reckon he mought; I h'aint heered uv you a-makin' no bad bets lately," and he accepted the dollar Jessie handed him in advance for ten shots.

At some distance from the men with guns there were a dozen chickens tethered a few feet apart on a line parallel to a line the marksmen were to shoot from. The chickens were at what looked to be some seventy-five paces or so out in the meadow. At about twenty-five yards farther out there was a line of eight or ten turkeys, five or six feet apart. The entrepreneurs of these events will not usually divulge the exact distances. This would give the participants a distinct advantage in setting their sights. Part of the game is to judge how much elevation the marksman has to allow in his aim. The twenty-two-caliber rifles that are mandatory for the contest are not very accurate at distances of more than fifty yards or so, and most contestants, if successful at all, have to fire a good many shots to win a turkey, or even a chicken. The fees were five cents a shot at the chickens and ten cents at the turkeys. Most of those competing would pay a good deal more than the market price for their prize— that is, if they won one; the majority would spend their money in vain. These are the odds that made holding a turkey shoot so attractive for the operator.

Incidentally, the "turkey shoot" is an American institution established in early Colonial times. The name is properly applied to any contest of marksmanship in which turkeys are used as prizes. This means there are no fixed rules applied and that there are almost as many varieties as there are locations or areas where these contests are held. The two main varieties are distinguished by the types of targets that are used. In one, the turkeys themselves are shot at. In the other, the target is some kind of bull's-eye applied to a solid backing that will show the location of bullet holes and their relative proximity to the center of the target. The winner is the one who makes the highest score on his target, whatever its type.

But in most areas the turkey shoot is not only a contest but also a social celebration to be enjoyed by any or all members of the community where it is held. In some communities, turkey shoots often occur on Independence Day and Thanksgiving Day, as part of the festivities. In eastern Kentucky they sometimes require no special occasion, and one may run onto one quite unexpectedly in any area. However, turkey shoots are always premeditated, as they require some planning and preparation. Fortunately, although alcohol is almost always present in the crowd, apparently there never had been much violence at turkey shoots in the area where the present one was being held. A traditional spirit of fun and camaraderie seemed to prevail, and there was a lot of banter and good-natured kidding among the contestants.

There were a few Bereans present, but I was unknown to nearly everyone there. They were predominantly citizens of Rockcastle County, and it was soon recognized that I was new to those parts. But one of the other shooters, a young fellow with a shock of red hair, approached me with a smile and said I had been pointed out to him in Berea. He said he was told I was "an artist." He wanted to know if he could come up sometime to the studio over the bank to see my work. He said he liked to draw pictures but had never painted any. Of course I gave him an invitation and asked him to bring some of his drawings. His name was Elmer Abner, a good Kentucky name, and I looked forward to his visit. He had a most interesting face.

Before I lined up to shoot, I watched the others for a while and studied the terrain. While I watched, two chickens and a turkey were apparently hit. Each time, all shooting was stopped while the shooter and one of O'Dell's boys went out to retrieve the prize. In the case of one chicken the bird had been killed outright. The other chicken and the turkey had to be inspected carefully to find the bullet wound, or to determine if the bird had simply flopped its wings at a near miss.

This was the case with the other chicken, and it was left in place as a continuing target; but the turkey had very obviously been hit, though not killed. This didn't matter as far as the shooter was concerned; since an outright kill was not required, he had won the prize.

This was not my first turkey shoot, and I had learned something from my experience. I had found that one should pick some spot in the background at which to aim, at the proper estimated elevation above the turkey. This is more accurate than just trying to hold the muzzle of the gun at the right height above the target. One could never see in the grass of the meadow where a bullet struck. The only clue to its trajectory would be some action of the target itself if the bullet came very near or actually struck it.

At my first shot I was sure I had approximately the right elevation when I saw the turkey jerk its head slightly. The second and third shots, aimed at the same spot in the distant background, brought no response from the turkey. The next shot, aimed just a bit lower at the spot in the distance, broke the bird's neck, as evidenced by its violent flopping for a full minute or so. That I knew was just luck, as I was still aiming a bit too high for the turkey's body. I refrained from pointing this out to any of the several who came over to congratulate me. But one of these, a sharp-looking old man, said to those gathered around me and the dead turkey, brought in by one of O'Dell's boys, "Aye God! That feller's a damn fine shot. Jist look whur he hit it at. He didn't want to spile the meat so he shot it thru the neck."

He regarded me with a meaningful grin and a twinkle in the eye that said plainly he knew it was just a lucky shot. I acknowledged his false tribute with a smile and a wink, and we became instant friends by mutual tacit understanding.

Jessie was surprisingly enthusiastic over "our" success. He even bought me a cold 7-Up when I told him I didn't want to try to win a turkey for myself. This meant his turkey cost him just forty cents! I had no need for a turkey myself, but I did have another reason for not shooting—I didn't want to "spile" my reputation in Rockcastle County as a "damn fine shot."

We stayed another half-hour or so to witness another chicken and a turkey won. We then made an uneventful return to Berea, with Jessie haranguing Junior all the way for driving without the slightest reference to his father's commands. We got there before noon, and I was able to put in a good afternoon on the Hagerstown job.

CHAPTER 9
Family Matters

IT SEEMS IN RETROSPECT that time in my life has always passed at disconcerting speed. I realize fully, now that I am in the late twilight years, that time's escape during my early life was nowhere near as rapid as it has become today. The less time remaining, the faster it flees away. But during the period I am writing about I remember being aghast at how much time had escaped with so little accomplished of the kind of work I wanted to do. There was always a feeling of guilt that I was making so little headway in my struggle to succeed as an artist. At times, when I was in an optimistic mood, I would reason that I was moving along as rapidly toward a successful career as could be expected under the circumstances. But more often, I would sink to near depression when I would feel that I had not worked as hard as I should have toward the success I believed I was capable of achieving.

This feeling was intensified when my father died in 1938. It had been ten years since I had finished my formal art education in 1928, and I had always hoped I could accomplish something during his lifetime to justify the faith he had in me and the sacrifices he and my mother had made to help assure my success. Actually, he had the delusion that I was well on the way to fame. He magnified the importance of everything—of every commission I received—and I am sure he died content with his delusion. That made the truth easier to accept, perhaps, but no less accusing.

The fact that he died as the result of an accident while still healthy and vigorous at seventy-eight was certainly no comfort. He was on his way to visit my brother in his office on an upper floor of a tall building in Knoxville when it happened. At that time, most elevators were operated by an attendant who pulled a lever down to open the heavy door so that passengers could enter and exit. Just as my father stepped out at my brother's floor, the handle slipped out of the operator's hand and the door closed on my father, striking him a heavy blow and pinning his body in the opening. Taken to the hospital for examination and treatment, he was later released in my brother's care, but he soon developed pneumonia. In those days, the miraculous drugs that are now an almost sure cure for the disease did not exist.

I was notified, and I drove to Knoxville immediately. When I reached his bedside he recognized me, smiled, and squeezed my hand. I could not believe he was near death, but the next morning I was called to his bedside and was holding his hand, my tears falling on his bed, when he breathed his last shallow breath.

It was a difficult time for all of us—most of all for my mother, who lost her lover and companion through the many years of ups and downs they had experienced together. We—my mother, brother, and I—decided she should remain with my brother and his family until I could make arrangements for her to come to Berea and live with me. I was very happy with this decision because I felt it was now my duty to take on this responsibility. My brother had contributed to our parents' welfare for the past several years while I was financially unable to do my share. Mother had received a considerable settlement from the accident insurance coverage of the building where the accident occurred, and this made our proposed arrangement possible. Of course I was unable to speculate about my financial future and how much responsibility of that sort I might be able to assume. My prospects did not seem very bright at the time.

Back in Berea, I was not long in locating a furnished house for rent that would satisfy our requirements. I then went to Knoxville for Mother, and we were soon installed in our new home. Preoccupation with these matters delayed work on the Hagerstown murals, of course, but there was enough time left on my contract to prevent any real concern on that score.

In spite of her great sense of loss, my mother adjusted remarkably well to the new situation. This ability to adjust was one of her most admirable qualities, and one quite necessary in living with my father, who was forever changing the family's location. It was not long before she was made welcome by my friends and by several neighbors. I thought it remarkable that at her age she was able to attract new friends in such a different environment and so soon after my father's death. But she had always had many friends, attracted by her conversational ability. She had a fund of stories about her early life and the many amusing situations she had experienced both during her early youth and in her life with my father. She was always willing to share these with friends. She also had a ready wit, which she had often turned on my father, who had become somewhat forgetful and repetitious as he aged. I remember overhearing him asking her one day if he had ever told her of some happening in his past. She answered wearily, "Well, not lately."

I also remember her answer to a woman she barely knew who, each time they met, would ask how many children she had. Finally she replied, "Actually, I counted them again this morning and found I still have just two."

The house we rented, on Crescent Drive, was owned by Dr. Cornelius, an optometrist with an office on Main Street. He lived next door to the one we rented from him. Crescent Drive is a very short, one-block-long street, and most of its few houses were owned or occupied by people connected with the college. The next house to ours on the other side from Dr. Cornelius belonged to Charles Price and his wife, Sallie, and their two small children. Charles was the head of the Berea College agriculture department.

It was during this period of living with Mother that I was called on to speak to several audiences about my work and the status of American art, particularly that which was generated by programs of the federal government. I had not done much public speaking, but fortunately I found I had a little natural aptitude and was fairly successful in interesting audiences in what I had to say.

One of my first invitations was to speak at one of Berea college's chapel programs. I was pleased by this opportunity. It gave me a chance to become known by the student body and the faculty, only a few of whom I knew personally at that time. I remember that when I ended my speech I was greatly surprised at Dean Shutt's congratulating me and handing me an envelope containing an honorarium check for my effort.

On another occasion I spoke to the Lexington Brush and Pencil Club at Ted Rannells's home. This involved talking about various media that amateur artists might use successfully. I also spoke to the Louisville Woman's Club and to the Kentucky Teachers Convention in Louisville.

There were a few other occasions, but the speech I shall never forget was given to the Fine Arts Society in Ashland, Kentucky. I believe this was the last speech I delivered before my career as a muralist was ended. To my great surprise I discovered that the president of the sponsoring organization was a former classmate of mine from my high school art class in Knoxville. Unfortunately, at this late date I can no longer recall her name, nor can I find it by trying to research the time and the scene, although I clearly recall other details. I remember that this invitation to speak also involved acting as judge of an exhibition of work by members of the organization.

Everything went well until that evening when I started getting ready to leave the hotel for the lecture hall. I had been somewhat apprehensive when I learned beforehand that the lecture and the preceding dinner were to be formal affairs. (Ashland is a sort of highbrow community.) I did not own a tuxedo, and of course there was no place in Berea to rent one. Naturally, I was elated when my good friend Abby Scruggs, a Berea insurance agent with an office on Short Street, offered to lend me his outfit. He was about my size and build, and we found that the tuxedo was an almost perfect fit. He was good enough to put it all in a package, which I placed in my travel bag.

When I unpacked, shortly before time to leave for the dinner, I was aghast to find that Abby had forgotten to include the suspenders! Of course there was a cummerbund, but there was nothing to hold up the trousers, which were not provided with loops for a belt. I called the porter. He was most accommodating and sympathetic. The only solution he could suggest was to attach the trousers to the shirttail with some very large safety pins, which he provided. These he pinned carefully, two in front, two in the rear, to hold the trousers at the right height for the cuffs to just clear the ground. This seemed to work satisfactorily during the dinner, but I found that during the lecture, while I was standing, the trousers began a very perceptible descent toward the floor. (Later, when I undressed I discovered we had done a poor job of fastening the pins. They were set horizontally, but not firmly enough to prevent their turning toward the vertical and allowing the trousers to slip downward by more than two inches.) Fortunately, I was standing behind the rather bulky lectern on which rested the text of my speech. Since this hid the lower two-thirds of my body from the audience, they could not see that the white shirt was gradually appearing in an increasing gap between the top of the trousers and the lower edge of the cummerbund. Nor could they see that the trouser legs were beginning to drape over my shoes! The fact that I knew this was happening did nothing toward putting me at ease in the delivery of my message. It was helpful that I was reading the speech rather than speaking ad lib—my usual practice. The newspaper that was covering the speech had let me know that it was to be broadcast by the local radio station and would have to be exactly forty-five minutes in length. I had thought (mistakenly) that the only way to achieve this was to prepare a written text and time my reading of it.

Somehow I was able to get through what became something of an ordeal. I managed to pull the trousers up from time to time with one hand, while disguising this maneuver by oratorical gestures with the other hand. I had pretty well memorized the speech and could appear not to be reading it word-for-word. When it was finished several people came up on stage to congratulate me. Apparently no one was aware of my problem. If it was noticed, possibly my covert grappling with my waistline from time to time suggested that I was simply scratching a persistent itch.

It was during the period of living with my mother in the rented house that I found an opportunity to do a lot of rabbit hunting. Our location was ideal for keeping rabbit hounds, and I was inspired to try to acquire a beagle hound to accompany me on my forays. There was none available in the Berea area; I had to be content with ordering one by mail, although this was somewhat chancy. Perusing the ads in hunting magazines, I ordered a beagle named Jack from a kennel in Illinois. I was very pleased when he arrived. He had the appearance of good breeding, and we soon became close in our relationship of hound and master—closer than usual, no doubt, because of two incidents that happened very soon after his arrival. In fact, the first occurred just the next day when I took him to an area fairly close to town to try him out. This was an area where I had hunted before, but without a dog. I knew the terrain and its rabbit population fairly well. I turned Jack loose from a rise in the ground where I could stand and watch him work. It was not long before he started a rabbit and began baying while following the scent. After a circuitous chase the rabbit came close to where I was standing. At that point I heard a sudden yapping and saw two dogs streaking from a farmhouse across a creek in the near distance. I had not known before that there were dogs living there. I did know the owner of the land bordering the creek on the side where we were hunting and had obtained his OK. The other dogs were trespassing, so to speak.

Jack was properly oblivious until the dogs almost caught up with him fairly close to where I stood. I called him, and he came at once followed by a shepherd and a pit bulldog growling insults. Beagles are not known as fighters—besides it was two on one if it came to that. So Jack came to heel and we started to leave the scene. I had gone only a few steps, thinking Jack was following, when I heard the fight start behind me. Evidently Jack, apparently sure I would back him up, had gone back in response to some unforgivable insult. I got to the scene in two jumps, but not before the bulldog had Jack by the throat, with the shepherd trying for a hold. The shepherd ran, but the bulldog had a death grip that he would not loosen in spite of blows from my rifle barrel. I saw the only hope was a final blow to the skull with the gun butt, which killed the dog instantly. Jack's throat was ripped open deeply, but fortunately the jugular was not broken, although there was a lot of bleeding. I wrapped the neck tightly with my large bandanna and carried Jack to the car not far away. When I reached a vet, Jack's throat was sewn up, and with medication and rest for several days he soon recovered. It was very apparent after this that Jack positively adored me as his protector—nay, his savior!

The other incident, which must have confirmed this impression for Jack, was of a different nature. The street on which Mother and I lived bordered on a cow pasture of several acres. Just across from us on the edge of the pasture was a sheltered spot—a perfect place for a doghouse where no one would object to our keeping Jack. He normally spent a lot of time in the pasture during the day trailing an occasional rabbit on his own, but he never wandered away any further than the pasture during night or day. One evening, however, he did not return from the pasture for his dinner. I called and whistled for him all around the pasture, and I visited the far reaches of the neighborhood asking if anyone might have seen him. The next morning he was still gone, and he did not appear during the day.

On the following morning I again searched the pasture. At its extreme tip I suddenly thought I heard a faint bark. At first it seemed a long way off, but circling near a dense patch of briers and weeds I realized the faint barks were coming from its center. After a difficult struggle to reach their source, I saw Jack hanging upside down, a hind leg caught in the two upper strands of an old barbwire fence that at one time had apparently marked the boundary of the pasture. With great effort and many scratches, I finally reached Jack. I had to pick him up bodily and lift him over the fence to release the pressure of the wires, which were holding his leg in a scissors-like grip. No doubt he had gotten caught trying to jump the wires while following a rabbit through the brier patch. He had hung there for two nights and three days—that is why his bark was so weak it sounded far away. He had bitten off all the brier stalks within his limited reach. Days later, I discovered a piece had become jammed crossways in the roof of his mouth. The whole experience must have been a terrible ordeal for Jack, but I'm sure that for him it proved again that I would be his savior in any crisis. Of course he received a lot of loving care from my mother and me until he was fully recovered.

Hunting with beagles is a great sport, especially if one uses a rifle instead of the more popular shotgun. The rabbit, not particularly alarmed at being followed by the slow-trailing beagle, always circles back to near where it was jumped. The hunter has only to stand near that spot until the rabbit appears, hopping slowly and stopping frequently, but never allowing the dog to get closer than forty or fifty yards. Thus, the hunter is offered a ridiculously easy shot. His greatest enjoyment is like that of the foxhunter listening to his pack of hounds pursue the chase. He does not always shoot the rabbit; he may refrain unless the rabbit is young and he wants it for food. And of course his pleasure is increased if he hunts with more than one hound.

That can explain why I bred Jack to a good beagle bitch that my good friend Howard Smith acquired later that same year. In place of a stud fee I received two pups of my choice from a litter of six. Their mother was well bred, but all except one female looked very much like Jack. I chose that one and one of the males. I named the female Molly and the male Jason. I derived great enjoyment from training them with Jack when they were about nine months old.

Like so many of my other interests, I came by this one "honestly," as the saying goes. My father raised bird dogs as far back as I could remember. The only difference was in the breed of dog I chose and the kind of hunting. I am glad to say, however, that I never went to the extreme of dropping all my other interests, even my livelihood, to indulge in the sport of hunting, as my father often did.

All during the changes in my life-style after my father's death, I continued work on the Hagerstown murals. But I also entered a Section competition for a mural in the Vicksburg, Mississippi, post office. Here again, I had no affinity with the area; I simply felt I had to take every opportunity offered to continue painting murals under this program in order to survive as an artist. I have stated that I never painted a historical subject, meaning one that depicted some specific, well-documented event. In this instance I chose a nonhistorical incident, but one that I knew was typical of occurrences in the period when this southern area was being populated. I called my design *Night Landing*. It showed a boatload of settlers landing at the Vicksburg site. The Section judges questioned the color scheme as being "unaccountably blonde," ignoring the fact that the scene was that of a *night* landing, as clearly indicated by the title, by a lighted lantern in the stern of the boat, and by the dark, unlighted background. I tried to convey an impression of moonlight, but unsuccessfully as far as the judges were concerned.

Still, although my design did not win the competition, I was awarded a contract for a mural in the Drumright, Oklahoma, post office as a result. As far as I can remember, no deadline was stated for the completion of this project; if there was one, it was not pressing. I was not long in finishing the Hagerstown mural and making an uneventful trip to Hagerstown by car with two assistants, my friend Chester Parks and one of the Neeley boys. We used the specified adhesive provided by the Section and finished installing the three panels in one full day.

I could not fathom why the Section had chosen me to do a mural as far out of my native territory as Oklahoma. I had no knowledge of the West, which I had never visited, and I felt I lacked any qualification that would fit me for that specific assignment. But I was not prepared to protest; I needed the job too much. (My familiar refrain when faced with the facts of life during the depression.) So I began searching for some subject that I could persuade myself to be interested in, in spite of my natural antipathy for illustration.

I could find nothing but the Oklahoma Land Rush, which occurred in 1889 when the then Territory was opened up for settlement. This was indeed interesting, and not too close to being a true "historical" incident to rule it out in my thinking. One hardly needed to have experienced it to visualize it quite realistically. I didn't know then, and don't know now, whether John Steuart Curry, a well-known illustrator of the day, painted his mural with this subject before or after I painted mine. No doubt his rendition was better than mine, since he was a professional illustrator, which I was not. Still, the Section seemed satisfied with the sketch I submitted for approval, and there was no mention of the Curry mural.

Some of my acquaintances found it hard to understand my aversion to working as an illustrator, or why illustration was considered a lower form of art than that which demonstrated less concern for the importance of subject matter. I tried to explain that the artist's freedom to express his originality is severely hampered if he is confined to an attempt to show, in another medium, what has already been revealed in literature or history with far greater accuracy than he can ever hope to achieve.

The painter as an artist is involved with the aesthetic possibilities of his medium in his concern with pure form and the relationship of form to color, as well as all the other abstract relationships among the elements of his art. The illustrator has far less interest in these abstract elements. The importance of his work in the field of art is secure; it is simply of a different nature and not on the same level of creativity as that of what might be called the "pure" painter. In this sense "pure" painting is similar to pure, nonthematic music. (In connection with this distinction I have found some confusion over the meaning of the term *abstract*, even among professionals. Some seem to think it refers to a summary of subject matter, as used in a legal sense. Its true meaning in terms of art is that without reference to reality.) I was not a full-fledged abstractionist; I was interested, however, in searching for an original style that could represent aspects of natural and human subjects in ways other than realistic, something I knew I would never find while working as a muralist-illustrator.

In the sketch I submitted to the section, I imagined what the scene of hundreds of settlers, in covered and uncovered wagons and on horseback, might have looked like to someone involved in it. The scene itself could not have appeared much different from my

Cartoon for Oklahoma Land Rush, *Drumright, Oklahoma.*
Courtesy National Archives.

The completed Drumright, Oklahoma, mural (photo taken in studio).
Courtesy National Archives.

conception, although another artist, more interested in its realistic rendition, might have been able to represent it more convincingly. Regardless of this, it was acceptable to the Section. I do not remember any comments, either critical or commendatory, and I started work on the mural shortly after receiving approval. The work was done as usual in the studio, with the finished mural to be mounted later in its place on the wall of the Drumright post office. Alonzo and I stretched and prepared the canvas with an oil ground, as described for the other murals I did under the Section program. The one was for a small post office; as was common, the panel was to fit on an end wall above a door to the office of the postmaster. I believe its dimensions were approximately six by twenty feet. As I remember it, I was able to complete the mural in fewer than thirty days of actual work while also devoting some time to other paintings and other interests.

It was during this time that I became acquainted with Laura Whitis, who was to have a profound effect on my life. She was the sister of Sallie Price, our next-door neighbor. Laura was working for the Sales Promotion Office of Student Industries. She and her mother had come to stay with the Price family a little after Mother and I had moved into the house next door. Because we were barely acquainted with the Prices, we were not introduced at once to Laura and her mother. I, of course, was anxious to meet this most attractive young lady, but I could think of no way to arrange it that wasn't too obvious. Normally, this would not have deterred me in such a situation, but there was something that deterred me now that I could not explain. My mother, with her keen insight, was quite aware of my interest, though she never referred to it. I suppose she observed my maneuvers to catch a glimpse of "the girl next door" from our windows.

Well, it happened that Laura and I frequently walked down the street that led from Short Street to our respective domiciles at the same hour for lunch. I used to watch on Main Street near my studio until I saw this young lady come by on her way and, unknown to her, fall in at a discreet distance behind to follow her to our street.

I felt sure she was unaware of the surreptitious attention she was receiving until one day she stopped to admire a flower blooming near the street. She looked up, saw me approaching, and then made some comment to me about the remarkable beauty of the flower. This led naturally to our becoming acquainted and sharing the knowledge that we were living next door to each other. Surprise, surprise!

Laura admitted a long time later that she had been just as aware of me as I was of her from the very first day of my following her. I should have known—but I was strangely and uncharacteristically shy in this particular situation, and unable to think straight. I was at last learning what love at first sight is like.

Of course I had "gone with" several girls since arriving in the area, but there had never been any serious commitment, and nothing deeply emotional like this. This was a totally new and different experience, and one that was to have a profound effect on my life-style. .

CHAPTER 10
Three Kentuckians See the West for the First Time

WITH THE ADVENT OF MY MOTHER, my life was suddenly changed, both internally and externally. For one thing, I had to give up some of my favorite pastimes; I could no longer spend most evenings at the Manhattan Club. For another, I avoided most social drinking, knowing that Mother would not approve. She had experienced enough bad times with my father's sporadic weakness for drink, and I didn't want to renew her anxiety on that point. Of course I was not deliriously happy about the altered situation, but it was only a short time later that "the girl next door" entered the scene. That changed things again for the better. I was sure my new pattern of behavior would impress Laura more favorably than the old one would have; and now, I was far more interested in spending any available time with her than in renewing any old habits.

Besides, I began to think in different terms about almost everything. When I would think of doing something I enjoyed I would first consider whether or not Laura might also enjoy it and accept an invitation to join me in it. I was always delighted when she was willing, and especially pleased at the revelation that we often had the same tastes. But one of my greatest satisfactions came from finding that my mother was most favorably impressed with Laura, and that the feeling was mutual. This made our growing intimacy much easier and more enjoyable than it could have been otherwise.

We made many trips to Lexington together to visit the Nileses and other friends. Laura even enjoyed going hunting with the hounds and me and on fishing trips to nearby Silver Creek and other more remote waters. Of course there was speculation about our "affair" among our friends, as well as among the Berea population in general—with much talk of how "serious" it might be, its degree of intimacy, the possibilities of a scandalous outcome, and so on.

It may be surprising that we never discussed the subject of marriage. I know that each of us thought a great deal about it on our own,

129

but we both knew that under present conditions it was an impossibility. We each had the responsibility of a mother to take care of. While we each also, for the moment, could rely on a brother or a sister to act responsibly in any emergency, neither of us could willfully shirk our own responsibilities, at that time or in the foreseeable future.

At this point, it seems strange to me that I was apparently able to carry on my work in the studio as efficiently as ever, if not more so, during this period of change. I not only finished work on the Drumright, Oklahoma, mural, I also executed a whole series of woodcuts and wood engravings, had new paintings accepted in several national exhibitions, and entered three of the Section's mural competitions. Looking back, I can't imagine how I could have accomplished as much as the record shows during those years from 1938 to 1941.

Not long after I met Laura, I shipped the finished mural to Drumright and followed it with a crew to mount the mural in place in the post office lobby. This was in 1939. Although the mural itself was not particularly notable, the long trip to Oklahoma with my two native eastern Kentucky helpers and our brief experience with some native Oklahomans made this one of the most interesting projects of my whole career as a mural painter for the government.

Selecting my helpers was no problem; Alonzo was one, of course, and Slim Belcher was the other. Incidentally, Slim was the brother of Arnold Belcher, of "Legal Liquor, Ky." fame. There were two or three others who would have liked the opportunity, but Slim was the most interesting, and I knew he could be counted on to stay sober and do the work to my satisfaction. Both he and Alonzo were very excited over the opportunity to see "the West."

The trip was somewhere around eight hundred miles by the route I had mapped out. We would travel on Route 60 to Lexington and Louisville, through Cairo, Illinois, to Springfield, Missouri, then on Route 66 into Tulsa, Oklahoma. I believe Drumright is only fifty or sixty miles from Tulsa. We didn't make any plans regarding where we would stop overnight, and I cannot now remember where these stops were made or, in fact, how long the trip took each way. We agreed that we would be relaxed and enjoy the trip, since nothing dictated how much or how little time should be involved. After all, we wanted to see as much of the West as possible and enjoy it, without straying too far from our route.

We started very early one September morning in my comparatively new car, a Hudson Terraplane, the car I had bought the year before and paid for with poker winnings. It was in excellent condition. Slim, seeing it for the first time, exclaimed admiringly, "Well, man, that shore is a neat fix."

Slim had a sonorous nasal twang that sounded much like the last gasps of an ancient pipe organ. Everything he admired became a "neat fix." He had a flair for comedy, and somehow could charm the opposite sex with his buffoonery. As we drove through the little towns along our route, he would lean out the open window of the car to make amorous remarks to any pretty girl we might pass. His favorite greeting was, "Well, hello, love! Come live with me!" followed by loud guffaws, embellished with his infectious grin. In his late twenties, he was not bad looking in a rugged sort of way. Far from being offended, most of those accosted thus could not refrain from responding with gales of laughter at this amorous clown. At first, I was somewhat apprehensive, fearing that some male protector of one of Slim's targets, witnessing his approach, might try to forcefully cool his ardor. Fortunately, this never happened. I suppose it was obvious to everyone that it was all in fun.

But all was not completely free from unpleasantness. The weather, during the day, would become hot and steamy, and the car, even with all the windows open, was gradually permeated with a decidedly pungent, fetid odor. (Air-conditioning was not available in cars at that time.) We soon realized that Alonzo's feet were the source. Slim said, "My God, Alonzo, don't you never wash them feet? Them smells worser 'n ary skunk."

Alonzo was defensive. "Of course I wash 'em, but it don't do no good. That's jist the way they're made—been that way all my life. Doc Baker said some people jist cain't he'p it. But I'll stick 'em out the winder an mebbe that'll he'p your tender nose."

Well, that was at least a partial solution, and we learned to ignore what was left of the odor. So we traveled with the spectacle of two oversize feet sticking out one of the rear windows for the rest of the trip. This was not too uncomfortable for Alonzo: he had the whole rear seat to himself. The spectacle drew some amused attention from other travelers, of course, but of this Alonzo was blissfully unaware.

We stopped overnight at various motels along the way, preferring those in the smaller towns as being less expensive; very adequate and comfortable, in general; and, as Slim pointed out, "more friendlier." One thing we noticed was that the food was not noticeably different from what we were used to in the restaurants at home, until we hit a café that advertised Texas chili. Slim had to try it, of course, much to his disgust at its potent burning of the gullet and our amusement. For our breakfasts, Slim insisted we all start with his recipe for a "barnyard cocktail." This consisted of a jigger of whiskey (sour mash), a raw egg (mixed thoroughly with the whiskey), a shot of Worcestershire sauce, and a few drops of Tabasco. This he claimed would "open yore eyes," and he was certainly right! It seemed to be an education to the bartenders who mixed it for us, and properly appreciated by them. We all understood from the start, however, that there would be no serious drinking on the trip, except possibly the night after the project was finished. We would have to see about that at the time.

After leaving Louisville, we were all conscious of the change in the landscape from our accustomed hills and mountains to more level terrain. From there through the tip of Illinois and Missouri there was not much to delight the eye (at least mine) in viewing nature. When we finally reached Oklahoma, we were astonished at the number of oil wells, as manifested by those strange mechanisms that looked like prehistoric flightless birds, pecking interminably at the unyielding terrain. They were everywhere we looked on the monotonous plains. I had to explain to my companions what they were, and their importance to our country's economy.

Slim was baffled over how this seemingly ineffective pecking could possibly get any oil out of the ground. So I had to give a simplified explanation of how the pump worked. At the end I asked if he didn't consider that a pretty "neat fix," and he agreed that it was.

I believe it was before noon of the third or fourth day that we finally arrived in Drumright. We gave the town a cursory inspection before we had lunch at one of several cafés. We were somewhat disappointed that it was not much like our idea of what a western town should look like, based on impressions gained from watching many a western movie. But then I realized and pointed out that this was not the same West as Hollywood's; we were barely on the eastern edge of what was now considered the real West. There were few cattle for cowboys to drive. Most Indians stayed on their reservations, or had become assimilated into jobs in the oil fields and were not very noticeably different from the rest of the population. The town was an oil town so thoroughly that it was easy to imagine it smelled of oil.

At the post office, after meeting the postmaster, who seemed very pleased at the prospect of having his new building decorated with the mural, we went right to work preparing the wall to receive it. First, the paint on the wall had to be removed, before we could apply the adhesive. This had been shipped to Drumright by the Section. It was the same Alexander Abels formula that had been used on the other murals—malodorous and hard to apply. I had shipped the mural from Berea, removed from the stretcher frame and rolled on a heavy, six-inch-diameter carpet cylinder. The mural was painted on canvas given a flexible oil ground, which allowed rolling without damage to the painting.

The post office officials let us use their ladders and provided all the other equipment we needed, except for our brushes and other tools, which we had brought with us. They allowed us to work in the building until we were finished at around eight in the evening, as I remember it. The next day, when the post office opened, a small crowd soon gathered to view the mural. The postmaster introduced me to several of the viewers, most of whom seemed impressed with the painting. It seemed he had alerted some "important" citizens, including a member or two of the town council. (The mayor was out of town, he explained.) The story of the Oklahoma Land Rush was familiar to everyone, apparently, but none had seen it depicted before; my choice of subject seemed to have been a fortunate one as far as the community was concerned.

While the discussion about my work was going on in the mural end of the lobby, I noticed that, at a little distance, Alonzo and Slim were in conversation with two very comely young ladies and a veritable giant of a man I felt sure was an Indian from his complexion and aquiline features. Slim seemed to have made his usual impression. He brought the trio over and introduced them to me. The girls were gushy in their admiration of the mural, while the Indian was completely noncommittal.

The day happened to be a Saturday and the post office closed at noon, so we all left together shortly before that hour. I do not remember who invited whom, but somehow the six of us ended up having lunch together in some restaurant of our new acquaintances' choosing. During the meal it developed that there was to be a big dance that night and the three of us were invited to attend. We learned that the girls were Gloria and Luanne (no last names) and the Indian was Joe.

I was impressed by the speed with which my companions had gotten on such intimate terms with the town's young social set. In discussing this with them later, we all agreed that something seemed a little strange about our trio of newly made friends. The two girls talked and giggled a lot to each other, but the taciturn Indian, although he seemed intimate with both of them, never appeared to be more attached to one than the other. We wondered if they might be living together in what the French would call a ménage à trois. We learned that all three were employed by one of the oil companies—the girls in the business office, the Indian as a drill operator in the field.

They picked us up that evening at our motel and drove us to a large hall of some kind on the outskirts of the town where the dance was being held. It was just getting under way when we arrived. A dance band was playing some jazz music, and several couples were on the floor. On all sides of the dance floor there were tables and chairs, and to one side in the rear a bar had been set up with a bartender in charge. The crowd consisted of a mixture of townspeople, mostly young, but with a scattering of gray heads.

We sat at a couple of the small tables and started off with some highballs and cocktails and a discussion of the oil fields. For the first time, the Indian, whose full name was Joe Butcher, showed some animation, probably stimulated by the three drinks he had quickly consumed. Evidently, he planned to impress us with the importance of his job. He showed us his watch fob, a small replica of one of the drill bits he used. It was an intriguing little object with several interlocking rotary wheels, armed with teeth of tungsten carbide; the teeth, he explained, drilled through the rock and allowed the hollow shaft of the pump, after the hole was drilled, to reach the oil bed and pump the oil to the surface. He said that drill bits with man-made diamond teeth were just being introduced. These, he said, would drill at a faster speed and would last a good deal longer than the tungsten carbide bits.

This information was most interesting, but slightly out of place at the moment, and Joe soon turned his attention to the dance floor. He danced with several girls he apparently knew, as well as with both Gloria and Luanne. Alonzo, Slim, and I also danced with the two girls from time to time, but we joined Joe on the sidelines when the crowd became more and more rowdy. Arguments seemed to be breaking out every few minutes, but it was two women who started the actual violence. One grabbed the other's hair and swung her in a wide arc, which upset a dancing couple in the middle of the floor. General chaos followed.

My attention centered on Joe. He was breathing audibly. His big hands were clasping and unclasping as he watched the turmoil. He appeared to be trying to control himself, but suddenly gave up and dashed into the middle of the fray, grabbing men by the collar and flinging them to the floor indiscriminately. It was hard to tell whether he was engaged in breaking up the fight or was trying to promote it. Fortunately, the police appeared on the scene before he killed or maimed someone accidentally with his display of superhuman strength.

The police officers seemed used to such disturbances and had no trouble calming the whole scene down without arresting anyone. They treated Joe as a peacemaker trying to break up the fight, whether he was or not, and seemed to be well acquainted with him and his tactics. At any rate, the fighting was over and the dance was over. I was surprised to find it near midnight when our party finally left the scene and Joe and the girls deposited us at our motel.

The next morning we talked about starting for home. I was now anxious to get back for more than one reason. I did not like to be away very long because of Mother. She was in fairly good health, although very frail, but at her age there was always some anxiety about what could happen, although I knew she was in good hands with our friends and neighbors in case of an emergency. I also missed Laura a good deal more than I had expected to. But I soon discovered that both Alonzo and Slim would like to stay in Drumright another day. It seemed they both wanted a little more time with members of the opposite sex whom they had just met. In Slim's case it was a gal he had met at the dance. She had promised him a date for the following evening if he could stay over. With Alonzo, the gal was none other than Gloria, the more attractive of the two we had met with Joe, the Indian, at the post office. She had the day off on Monday and had promised Alonzo to spend the afternoon with him. I didn't like staying over, but I was swayed by my genuine liking for both of my helpers, who had managed to stay relatively sober through the entire trip, so I agreed to the delay. The next day, Slim told me confidentially that Alonzo was really smitten with Gloria, and because of this was planning to remain in Drumright when we left.

"Why, hell man," Slim said he had told Alonzo. "You cain't make no time with her. She's that there Indian's gal, an' you might git yorese'f killt—or at least beat to a frazzle. B'sides that, how you expect to start a-makin' a livin' out hyur? You know you got to tell anybody you hit fer a job that yore a ex-con. B'sides, what about yore parole officer back in Kentucky? Cain't you git yorese'f in a peck o' trouble 'thout checkin' with him?" But, as Slim reported to me, "He had some kinda answer to everthing I said. Hell, he h'ain't got no money 'cept what you'll give him. Hit's the biggest piece o' foolishment I ever heered a growed-up man come out with."

Slim said that one thing Alonzo seemed sure of was that the Indian wasn't sweet on Gloria. He claimed they were just friends. I told Slim not to worry—that I knew I could talk Alonzo out of it. If nothing else worked I would refuse to pay him until we were back in Berea—what we had agreed on at the start. So we left it at that.

That afternoon, Slim and I managed to get out to the oil field by taxi and spent several hours watching a drilling operation. We didn't know where to look for Joe's rig, or we would have tried to find him. But we both were fascinated with what we saw of the ingenious process of extracting this ages-old substance, which man has found so valuable today, from the remote recesses in the bowels of the earth where it was formed.

Alonzo had dinner with Slim and me after his afternoon with Gloria. He said they had gone to a movie and then walked around the town looking in store windows. He told about Gloria seeing a pair of "darling" red slippers in one of the displays. She admired them so much that Alonzo bought them for her.

It was at that point that I said I had heard he wanted to stay in Drumright if we left the next morning as planned. I simply said that that would not be at all practical from my standpoint—that I was counting on him to help drive back to Berea and that I would also need his help on my next mural job. I did not go into his personal problems, since Slim had already pointed those out to him. The clincher was that I would not pay him for his help on the trip until we got back to Berea. He was very obviously disappointed, but realized he had no option but to agree. With all his disappointment he wasn't bitter about my refusal to comply with his desire. He said he was glad he hadn't told Gloria anything about wanting to stay. He said she had told him she had a date for that evening, and he guessed he wouldn't get to see her again before we left next morning.

We were ready to start the return trip very early. We got up around 4:00 A.M., and Slim and I went to the café around the corner for breakfast. Alonzo said he would meet us there in a few minutes after he ran upstairs to Gloria's room in the hotel in the next block to say good-bye. Slim and I just looked at each other. Slim said gloomily, "He ain't nothin' but jist a kid."

We were surprised when he came into the café almost before we were seated. His face was a picture of disaster. No one said a word for some time. Finally, Slim said, almost politely, "Well, I reckon you told her good-bye, did you?"

Alonzo seemed not to have heard the question. He appeared to be looking out the window at something in the far distance. The waitress came and took our orders before he managed to reply. I gave him credit—his voice was almost normal when he said, "Well, I went up to her room. I hadn't told her I would. I opened the door—she never locks it. I walked in an' the first thing I seed was them little red slippers I bought her. They was right alongside of them big boots Joe Butcher wears. They was under the bed whur him an' her was a-layin' all snuggled up together."

There was a long pause.

Slim couldn't help it; I couldn't either. We exploded together in a burst of wild laughter we could not control. Give him credit again: Alonzo, in spite of the shock of his blasted illusion, could not fail to appreciate the tragicomedy of the situation, even though it was at his expense. At last, he had to sheepishly join in. We three shared an irresistible joke. Slim and I had to promise Alonzo never to tell the story to anyone in Berea. But I'm sure none of us believed we could keep that promise. Anyhow, ever after, in any glum situation, we had only to mention "them little red slippers" to set off howls of laughter among the three of us.

Retracing the route we had followed when we came west to Drumright was completely uneventful. At least my memory retains nothing worth writing about. I remember only that I was very happy to have made a successful trip and be ready to resume work in the studio. The experience in a different part of the country, short as it was, had made me realize how much I loved and missed the hills and forests of eastern Kentucky when away from them for even such a brief period as the trip to the near West had required. I would be so happy to be back home again with my mother, and with Laura.

CHAPTER 11
A Mural for Morehead, Kentucky

NOT LONG AFTER RETURNING FROM OKLAHOMA I was notified that as a result of the competition for a mural in the Richmond, Virginia, post office I had been awarded a commission for a mural in Morehead, Kentucky. I was not greatly surprised at not getting the first award. Although I had made a very earnest effort to win it, I had not been very enthusiastic about competing. I was becoming more and more dissatisfied with the situation that forced me to continue working in a program in which I had little faith as far as its ultimate creation of significant works of art was concerned. Painting one mural after another merely to make a living was threatening my artistic integrity. I had begun to resent having to spend so much time striving to win commissions in which I had so little artistic interest.

For the Richmond competition I had spent considerable time and energy in producing a scale model of the lobby of the post office showing my proposed design in place. This was very successful as a means of giving a realistic impression of how the mural would appear in relation to the architecture. But I was well aware that showing a farmer plowing a field and a boy approaching with a bucket of water to satisfy his thirst was a pretty trite concept. It seems in retrospect that I must have been counting on the Section's lack of artistic discrimination, which I had long been aware of, to find merit in the idea. I am not sure at this point whether or not I ever saw the winning design, so I cannot make any comparison. I fully realized that my only interest in that particular project was the fact that it offered a larger commission than the consolation prizes I had been winning in other contests. Now here I was again with just such a prize. Still, of course, it was a good deal better than nothing, financially at least.

The Morehead mural had a very flexible finishing date, so I was able to turn my attention to the subjects that I considered my legitimate creative work in various media. Although I don't remember precisely how these projects were fitted into periods of work on the Morehead mural, I remember that I completed a number of what I called "invented flower" paintings in egg tempera, as well as some woodcuts and engravings. I also painted a portrait of the infant Jonathan Edward Niles at the piano keyboard—a commission from the Nileses.

It was also during this period of 1939–1940 that I took every opportunity to be with Laura. But she had taken an office job in Richmond, Kentucky, working on a WPA public roads project there. She and her mother had moved to Richmond, which made our contacts a little less convenient. They were in Richmond for almost a year before Laura took a Civil Service exam for a position with the War Department in Washington, D.C. Laura was in Washington by herself for a short time until she could arrange for her mother to join her. That was sometime in 1941.

This unhappy turn of events, I am sure, was a more serious blow to me than to Laura, although she seemed deeply affected by it. Neither of us could be sure that this disruption of the course of our true love would not be permanent. It was a period of vast uncertainty for almost everyone in the world at large. Of course we wrote frequently, affirming our everlasting devotion to each other.

It was not long after this separation that the owners of my studio over the bank proposed a plan to remodel it by converting the smaller of the two rooms, with its closet, washroom, and storage space, into comfortable living quarters with bath, kitchenette, and all the conveniences. John Dean shrewdly calculated that I would approve this plan so that my mother and I could live together there for a good deal less rent than we were paying where we then lived. He was right, of course, and the move was made when the alterations were finished late in the year. I had wondered how Mother would feel about the move. Although it meant going up and down that long flight of steps, she seemed to accomplish that exercise with no trouble; with her natural but surprising adaptability she seemed to make the change with no difficulty at all.

Naturally, I had to make some adjustment. I could not bring my dogs and take care of them in the studio apartment, but fortunately I was able to continue keeping them across the street from the house we had occupied on Crescent Drive. The owner of the field where they could roam during the day had no objection, and I could go twice a day to feed and take care of anything else they might need. It was the hunting season, so the hounds and I were not at all unhappy with the minor alteration in our normal routine.

For the first time, I had some difficulties with Ed Rowan and the Section. It concerned my treatment of the figures in the sketch I submitted for Morehead. I did discover later, by the grapevine so to speak, that although he had never been critical before, Rowan was actually not very enthusiastic about the style of my work. With this submission, he let me know that he thought my rendition of the two females was not suitable. He felt the older of the two women was so unattractive and the younger so alluring by contrast that the local populace would find them highly unrepresentative and might resent this treatment. I could not agree with the criticism; I was sure that the people of the community would not be apt to find anything to object to in the portrayals Rowan referred to. Sue Bridwell Beckham, in her exhaustive work, *Depression Post Office Murals and Southern Culture: A Gentle Reconstruction*, quotes a letter from me to Rowan that she unearthed in the National Archives.

Regarding criticism of the two females in my sketch, I can only say I wish you people would come down to these parts and see for yourself the types of womenfolk we have. Generally the old ones have developed into living caricatures of what we might image when we think of old ladies; and the young ones, even on the farms, are pretty interesting to look at as regards pulchritude. Dress them in the latest styles, hide their hands and feet, seat them in a graceful pose, and I would defy anyone to distinguish them, at a distance of twelve feet, from something you might expect to have come off Park Avenue.

The secret of the difference here between youth and age is probably the hellish existence most of these mountain farmwives endure. It puts lumps where once were curves. If they happen to get fat, as did this old girl, the cause is glandular; not luxurious living. It was this contrast I had in mind when I so gaily made the sketch.

The rejected design for Rural Free Delivery, *Morehead, Kentucky.*
Courtesy National Archives.

The completed Morehead, Kentucky, mural (photo taken in studio).
Courtesy National Archives.

The only thing remarkable about this letter (besides its having been unearthed) is the fact that years later I had no memory whatever of having written it, or in fact of any disagreement concerning the mural! It was only when the letter was shown to me and I recognized my handwriting that I could believe the incident ever occurred. I have now come to understand that this is a manifestation of a well-known psychological phenomenon in which the individual erases from his memory an experience too painful or disagreeable to retain. I can believe this, because now that the incident has come to light, I am deeply ashamed of having capitulated in the face of the criticism and agreeing to make the changes that made the mural acceptable to the Section. I now feel that I sacrificed the aesthetic truth of what I saw and created for the sake of a material reward.

Through Sue Beckham's book I discovered what I had long suspected: that other artists in the program had difficulties with Rowan and the Section of a similar nature to those I experienced, and some much more severe than mine. It is small wonder that this program produced so little work of true artistic merit.

It was while working on the Morehead mural that I developed an idea for one of my most successful paintings of that period. One morning as I was walking up Main Street near my studio I saw an unfamiliar family approaching—man, woman, and child. The child was a baby less than a year old carried in its mother's arms. The man was small but rugged and wiry. He carried a battered suitcase with one hand and a bundle in a blanket with the other. The woman was beautiful in a totally unsophisticated sense. She could have been a model for Mary in a nativity scene by a Renaissance master. I could see clearly that they were not residents of the town and were probably from some remote area in the mountains to the east. I approached the group, smiling a greeting and saying, "You must be from out of town. What brings you to Berea?"

The man replied, "Yes sir, we air from back in Jackson not fur from Sand Gap. We got burnt out of our cabin yestidy. The far got started in the chimbly when I warn't thar. Burnt up all our house plunder an' nigh everthing else we had. We come on this mornin' to Berear a-lookin' fer work."

After commiserating with them I gave them directions to the Red Cross office in town, which I thought might assist them in some way.

Then I explained that I was an artist and my studio was just upstairs over the bank near where we were standing. I said I would like to draw their picture and would pay them a dollar if they would come upstairs and pose for about half an hour. The man instantly grabbed up his suitcase, which he had set down to talk, and we all climbed the stairs to the studio.

What I remember most about making the sketch was how still they posed without my prompting. I suppose they thought that taking a sketch was similar to using the slow film and lenses of the early cameras they had seen. My assurance that such rigidity was not necessary had no effect. Even the baby responded to the hissed warnings of its father and was remarkably still. I thought it rather strange that when I was finished, neither the man nor the woman showed the slightest interest in seeing what I had done. The man accepted the dollar with alacrity, and the family descended the long flight of stairs to the street and their hopelessness without comment. I remained at the top of the stairs for a long moment, lost in thought.

The painting I made from the sketch showed the family seated in front of the smoldering ruins of their cabin. Their desolation was subtly suggested in their attitudes and expressions. The work was first exhibited in one of the national art exhibitions in a New York gallery or museum whose name I have no record of. It was then chosen to represent the state of Kentucky in the New York World's Fair of 1939–1940 and the 1940 Golden Gate Exposition in San Francisco.

As successful as this and the other work I was doing at the time was, I was still striving to develop a more personal style that I hoped would achieve some recognition for its originality. I continued to chafe under the necessity to keep on entering the Section's competitions for murals in which I had little or no interest.

But my main concern after receiving approval of the changes I was forced to make in the Morehead sketch was to get the painting started and finished as quickly as possible, even though I was enjoying a period of freedom to work on more creative projects. I was able to do all the work on the mural in about two weeks. I used a chalk ground on the canvas to assist in creating a matte effect on the surface of the finished painting. I wanted to try this as a simulation of the effect of a true fresco, which is painted on damp plaster, although it meant I would have to crate and ship the finished work in its full dimensions, since the canvas could not be rolled. I was more interested in the subject of this mural, naturally, than I had been in those for murals I had tried for in other Section competitions for locations of which I had no personal experience or background knowledge. Still, I had to treat the painting as a mural—quite different from the far more personal style I would use in my "own" work. But the characters I used were types that I knew well by association, although as usual I used no models.

To install the finished painting, Alonzo and I left Berea early one Saturday morning and arrived in Morehead before noon. The road was good and the distance something less than a hundred miles. This was my first trip through this particular segment of the state, and I enjoyed the new scenery of wooded hills and open fields. I believe Alonzo did too.

I remember that at one point we were stopped at a railroad crossing to await the passage of a slow-moving freight train. I recall that as we watched the boxcars roll slowly by, Alonzo would read the long strings of numbers on each car. I asked why he did this. He said he just liked to remember numbers. These were numbers with as many as a dozen digits each.

"How can you do that?" I wanted to know. "How do you know you remember them right?"

"Well, I jist know it," he said, stubbornly. I was incredulous and showed it. But I wondered as well. I remembered that when we were talking about the trip to Oklahoma he appeared to recall, in detail, minor incidents and interesting things we saw along the road, which I had already forgotten. On that adventure, during the return trip to Berea he would frequently alert us to points of interest that were coming up ahead that neither Slim nor I had noticed when going in the other direction. I wondered if he could possibly have what is known as total recall.

We arrived at the post office in Morehead in late morning and were welcomed by the postmaster. He led us to the area where the crated mural was waiting for us; it had arrived by truck freight the day before. After uncrating it, we went to work at once preparing the wall to receive it.

Because of the special chalk ground I had applied to the canvas, it had to be handled with great care to avoid damage in affixing it to the base adhesive coat we had spread on the wall. We used post office stepladders and walk boards to ready the wall, then lifted the sheet of canvas into place. We needed a third set of hands to manage this, which was provided by the post office janitor. Once the canvas was in place, we used soft rubber rollers over the entire surface to assure its complete adhesion to the adhesive-coated wall.

We had chosen a Saturday for the installation so that with the cooperation of the postmaster we could work all afternoon while the lobby was not open to the public. When we were finished, I was pleased with the visual effect of the mural in place. It had the flat surface I had tried for in using the chalk ground to prepare the canvas. The postmaster, and everyone else who commented about the mural, seemed highly pleased with it, including those who later commented on it in local newspapers. Alonzo and I were gratified that everything had gone so well with the installation that we were able to return to Berea without having to stay overnight.

I was glad, as usual when completing a mural, to have a period of respite from work that I did not greatly enjoy. I could now afford to indulge my sporting instincts and do some squirrel hunting in the forested hills to the east. This, or rabbit hunting with the hounds, almost always renewed my creative energy and led to new inspirations for pictorial ideas.

One of the areas I used to hunt for squirrels was always a challenge of sorts. It was called the "dark holler" and was avoided by most hunters because it was known for containing rattlesnake dens. I could not confirm its reputation. I had visited it often and had encountered only one rattler. I did not share the somewhat morbid fear and dread these snakes aroused in the local residents. I would never kill one unless I felt it a danger, to myself or others, that could not be avoided with due caution. I feel sure the rumors of snake dens in that area were probably based on fact, but the snakes in unusual numbers were apt to appear only in the heat of summer during the mating season. I did not hunt squirrels during that period, but later in the fall.

The best time to hunt squirrels if you are really serious about it is early morning. Getting in place before daylight is best, but on this particular day in early September I decided rather suddenly to hunt in the afternoon of a rather warm day. For some reason I have forgotten I chose to hunt the dark hollow. I drove a couple of miles to reach a spot from which I could hit the trail to my destination shortly after entering the forest.

I had been walking the trail that led to the hollow only a few minutes when I met a rather strange-looking character going in the opposite direction. I recognized him through having seen him occasionally walking the streets in town. The most notable aspect in his appearance was his extremely powerful build. He looked like a professional weight lifter. He was rather short in stature, with broad, muscular shoulders bulging under his thin shirt, wet with sweat. His short, bowed legs were equally muscular. I had been told he was a deaf-mute, named Ollie Nero, who lived alone in a cabin somewhere in the vicinity surrounding the dark hollow. He looked to be near thirty. He was very friendly with everyone, grinning and gurgling the strained, guttural sounds that he apparently hoped his graphic gestures would translate into words. It was generally concluded that he was somewhat mentally defective.

I was as startled to meet him so suddenly as he was to meet me, apparently. We almost came face-to-face in the narrow, overgrown path before we saw each other. But he immediately started grinning and gurgling. He was leaning somewhat forward, and his right hand seemed to be carrying something over his shoulder. He appeared to be greatly excited, and his eyes flashed as he dropped in the path between us the biggest rattlesnake I had ever seen. He had been carrying it by its head, its body hanging down his back. Of course it was quite dead, but it still feebly writhed spasmodically. I guess my astonishment was apparent. He went into a frenzy of gestures in an attempt to describe how he had killed it. He carried no gun that I could see, so I had to conclude he had used some other kind of weapon.

It seemed he could read the question in my eyes; he went off the path and found a stout stick. With this he pointed to the snake and then beat the ground energetically. I could see the snake's head was beaten to a pulp. Then, with graphic gestures he demonstrated clearly how the snake would coil and strike, and how he would persuade it to strike again and again with the stick, keeping safely out of range of its fangs. He was using the technique I had once seen a cat use in a similar fight with a snake—gradually wearing the snake out to the point where its strike was slow enough to allow a swift attack on the extended head before it could be withdrawn to strike again. I was greatly impressed, not just with the snake, but with the man's histrionic ability as revealed by such a convincing performance. With this same talent he made me understand he was taking the snake somewhere to have it measured. He clearly thought it was some kind of record in size, and I agreed. It was sometime later that I heard the snake measured slightly over six feet in length at Wrenn's Store on Scaffold Cane, and this was indeed a record for the state as a whole. It was a timber diamondback, *Crotalus horridus*, a species that does not rival the Florida eastern diamondback, *Crotalus adamanteus*, which has been registered at lengths as great as eight feet.

I believe it was more than a few years later that I heard the horrifying news that Nero had committed suicide. I think this was after the war when I returned to Berea from the army. His body was found in his well, feet uppermost, with his head underwater, indicating he had dived—it appeared he could not have accidentally fallen into the shaft of the well. Nobody knew much about the man who lived alone in a very sequestered spot in the woods and came to town only infrequently. I thought a lot about the sad case of this poor soul who lived in such desperate isolation because of an affliction that he finally could no longer bear to live with.

I remember that after my meeting with him I continued my course to the dark hollow wishing I could hear a more complete account of the killing of the rattlesnake. Since this was in the early fall, it was not uncommon for the snakes to come out into the sun before hibernating for the winter. I wondered if Ollie actually hunted the snakes in the hollow for food (they are excellent eating when properly prepared) or if he had encountered this snake by accident. I would never know.

I saw no more rattlesnakes that beautiful day, and only two squirrels, just one of which I bagged. But I enjoyed the outing in the pleasant surroundings of foliage barely beginning to change color. And I enjoyed, as always, the fragrance of the forest—the smell of damp moss (it had rained the night before), the rare perfume of early fall blossoms, and the slight pungency of dead leaves and various fungi, overturned by my feet as I walked. I returned to my studio and to work, greatly refreshed and energized, with a desire to create newly conceived images in my search for a completely original approach and style.

CHAPTER 12
A Competition Is Held for a Mural in Berea

AT SOME POINT DURING THIS LULL in my work as a muralist, I received an announcement from the Section of Fine Arts for another competition. This was a national competition for a number of panels to decorate the walls of a new federal building in St. Louis, Missouri. As usual, I felt compelled to enter due to the economic concerns I have frequently described, in spite of my lack of knowledge of the area involved. Probably because of my equal lack of interest in the prospect of another mural project, I am now completely unable to recall what subject matter I dug out by research, or what any of the sketches I finally submitted looked like. I think I probably spent a minimal amount of time on them, then dismissed them mentally.

But I do remember that not long after this another competition was announced for a mural in our Berea post office. This was something of a surprise, since competitions for the decoration of federal buildings were not usually held for towns the size of Berea. In this instance, the competition was the result of an effort by several Berea citizens that was first stimulated by an erroneous news article that appeared at the time the mural project for the Louisville post office was announced. The careless writer seemed to have misread the location as Berea simply because I had been selected to do the work. But apparently the mistake did implant the idea that Berea should have its own post office mural.

I am sure that Mary Ela, head of the Berea College Art Department, was responsible for making the request to Washington, which stressed the extent of the local interest and the number of Kentucky artists likely to be interested in competing. At any rate, the request was considered to have merit and was approved by the Section of Fine Arts. A local committee was formed to judge the entries and recommend the winner to the Section. Mary Ela was appointed chairman. She directed the proceedings of the committee and acted as liaison with the Section.

For my part, I was fully enthusiastic over a project for almost the first time in my association with the Section's program. I felt confident that I would be able to find an appropriate subject for my entry, and one in which I would have great interest because of my acquaintance with the area, the people, and their culture.

I believe this was an unusual situation. It was exceptional to find professional artists practicing their art in towns as small as Berea. If this were not the case, it seems obvious that local, qualified artists would have been chosen more often to undertake projects of this sort. The fact that I lived in Berea might seem to indicate that I could have had an inside advantage in this competition, and I guess this is true in spite of the fact that there were two other professionals in the immediate area who could be expected to enter. These were Joe Cantieni, an art teacher in the college art department, and Bert Mullins, my former pupil and assistant on the Louisville mural project. Joe seemed highly qualified, except for the fact that he had never painted a mural, and Bert had been entering these competitions of late with some encouraging responses from the Section. The competition was statewide, and it was thought other professionals in the larger cities might also be interested. However, the money award, which I remember to have been only $800 (the award was the same for all projects of this class, I believe), was not too attractive, although during the depression this was not an inconsiderable sum for most artists.

Although I had thought, erroneously, that the Section was first conceived especially to aid those professional artists who could not qualify economically for the assistance offered by the WPA projects, nonprofessionals and some rank amateurs often entered its competitions in the hope that their entries might be chosen. The quality of some of the murals chosen by the Section's judges bears witness to the fact that this did indeed happen. It also is a strong indication that the critical competence of the Section's judges is to be seriously questioned. I sometimes wondered if the Section's motive had become helping unknown artists, rather than the professionals I had first assumed.

Of course I went to work at once on the task of finding an appropriate subject. Oddly enough, as it turned out, it was while talking with Bert Mullins's father one day that I heard, for the first time,

Design for An Old-Time Berea Commencement, *Berea, Kentucky.*
Courtesy National Archives.

The completed Berea, Kentucky, mural.
Photograph by M. S. Rezny.

how commencement day for Berea College used to be celebrated by the town. This well-nigh unique celebration, as described by Mr. Mullins and other old-timers whom I talked with later, was the largest, most joyful and convivial gathering of the whole year. It was not confined to the families who had offspring or other kin, or merely friends, in the graduation ceremony itself—it attracted people from a very large part of eastern Kentucky, and even a few from other Appalachian states. Besides those who came to attend the graduation itself, many from the surrounding area came for other reasons and purposes. It was a great occasion for social mingling—a time for renewing acquaintances or for other activities. There were always those who came to swap pistols, pocket knives, horses, and what-have-you, including stories. Not to be sanctioned or discussed were those who came bringing moonshine liquor to imbibe or to sell or trade surreptitiously.

Most of the participants who came brought along their own food, but there were also open-air stands where such items as sandwiches, lemonade, and above all, bananas were available. This last item—almost unknown at any other time or place during those years—was so popular that the celebration came to be known in the region as "banana day." There was an oft-told story about a man from the mountains who came to this occasion for the first time. When he was offered a banana he said, "So that's a banana I've heerd so much about. No thanks—I won't taste it. I've got so many tastes now I cain't satisfy I'd better not take on another'n."

All of these activities took place in the open air, under the trees that shaded most of the campus. The area used was adjacent to the Tabernacle, a building constructed of wood in a still earlier period for a religious revival of some kind and later used for the commencement exercises. People came to this location in wagons drawn by teams of horses, mules, and sometimes oxen. They came riding single beasts of these same species. Some came a day, or even two days, before the event and camped on the grounds.

In my design I tried to depict these activities as accurately as I could envision them. Today, I cannot imagine why I did not do a better job of it. The mural I eventually executed in the post office fails to show the swarming nature of the crowds that must have occupied the scene. There are not enough actors in this pageant; not enough children;

not enough beasts or vehicles; in short, not enough of anything to show what must have been the crowded appearance of the scene.

This is my own evaluation; I never heard anything similar from others—not even from the few old-timers still able to remember what the actual commence day was like. It is possible, of course, to rationalize the effect by imagining this to be a view taken of an early stage of the gathering before the full crowd had assembled. I might appreciate that interpretation if I could not now see clearly how much better the mural could have been.

Surprisingly, I had no criticism or other difficulties from the Section concerning either the sketch submitted or the mural itself painted on the wall of the post office. It was only from other sources that I heard Ed Rowan's observation that my people were "wooden" and the foliage of my trees "stiff." Perhaps defensively, I had to conclude he didn't quite understand the difference between naturalistic effects and stylization.

In studying the architecture of the setting, even before I chose the subject to paint, I could see that something with many elements on a small scale would be more suitable visually than a design with larger figures. Because of a vestibule protruding into the lobby, a complete view of the mural would be available only from a relatively short distance away. After determining this, I decided to construct a small-scale model of the lobby showing a simplified rendition of the proposed mural in place. This helped to crystallize my own conception, and I felt it would help to convince a jury of my competence.

After the submission of the designs, there was a considerable waiting period before anything happened in connection with the project. It was during this lull that I received a major shock to my equanimity. I was notified by the Morehead postmaster that the mural there had fallen off the wall! I could not imagine why, unless the adhesive mix provided by the Section was at fault. I knew this meant that the painting was ruined beyond repair. Because of the friable nature of the chalk ground, the paint would have suffered many visible as well as invisible cracks. I immediately broke the news of this minor disaster to Ed Rowan and stated my belief that there must have been something defective in the batch of adhesive sent to the site by the Section for my use.

I cannot recall how much time and negotiation was involved in settling the matter. In the end it was decided that I would be paid the amount of the original contract to produce an exact duplicate and install it, using the traditional white lead as an adhesive.

I was very unhappy over this most discouraging development. I derived no satisfaction whatever from being paid twice for the same job. I doubt that any sensitive artist could be anything but revolted by the overwhelming, unredeeming drudgery of such a task. Of course I had no choice but to comply if I expected to continue working for the Section for my daily bread. But fortunately, I was successful in setting my own deadline for completing the new contract, and I gave myself enough time to finish a few other more agreeable projects of my own. When I felt able I went to work on the disagreeable task and managed to complete it in a good deal less time than the original had required. Rather uncharacteristically, I had preserved the cartoon for this mural, and of course this saved the duplication of a lot of work and made an exact copy more possible.

When the new mural was finished and shipped, Alonzo and I went to Morehead and duplicated almost exactly the entire process, described previously, of installing the canvas. The trip, as far as I can remember, was without any significant incident. I know I was greatly relieved when I could put the whole unfortunate experience behind me and get on with more creative work.

I think it was something of a coincidence that right after our return to Berea, I happened to meet Jim Taylor on the street. He was one of Alonzo's former cronies, and in response to a question about Alonzo I was telling him about our two trips to Morehead. It was when I happened to mention Alonzo's preoccupation with those long numbers on the boxcars at the railroad crossing that he started laughing. He then described a similar incident that had happened a long while before. He said he and Alonzo were once stopped, while driving, at a railroad crossing very close to Berea, and Alonzo went through the same maneuver with the numbers on the passing cars that I had just described. Sometime later in Berea, as Taylor told it, they happened to see that the same train had left some of its cars on a siding there. He said he challenged Alonzo about remembering the numbers on the cars. Before they approached near enough to read the numbers on the cars themselves, Alonzo wrote down the long strings of numbers as he remembered them from each car on the train, in the order of their passing. When they walked to the track where the cars stood, he triumphantly showed that the numbers on these few cars were included on the list he had written down! Taylor said he was amazed and puzzled. "I couldn't figger out how he done it—musta had some kinda gimmick. But hit didn't seem like hit was good fer nothin' I could think of. I don't think he could git no job jist because he could do it."

I thought that might not be true, although I didn't say so. I had barely heard of "total recall" (which I thought this appeared to be) as a little-understood mental phenomenon that I was sure could be a tremendous asset in the education of anyone fortunate enough to possess it. And I thought how unfortunate it was that Alonzo's teachers, in the comparatively little education he had received, had not been able to discover and develop this talent for his ultimate maximum benefit. I supposed it might be this singular ability that I had somehow sensed when I thought he had some mental quality that set him above his background.

At last the local committee announced there would be a showing in the college art gallery of the designs submitted for the post office mural. There were eleven entries, including three from Berea itself. If I ever knew the names of the nonlocal contestants, I have now forgotten them. Probably most, if not all, came from Lexington or Louisville, as there were several professional artists in both cities. The winning entry had not yet been selected by the committee. Apparently, the judges wanted to gauge the reaction of the town to the entries before making their final decision.

My faulty memory can recall only one of the designs besides my own. This was the one submitted by Joe Cantieni, and it was the one I would have selected in preference to my own if I had been a judge. It was an excellent abstract construction of assembled elements that I believe represented the architectural layout of the community. I knew of course that it would have no chance of approval by the Section, and I imagine Joe knew, too, but didn't care, thus remaining true to his own artistic vision.

I have only a vague recollection of Bert Mullins's design. I believe it was a representation of the area landscape, showing forested hills and open farmland, but this could have been some other artist's entry.

Bert had made considerable progress as a muralist in the previous year or so after giving up his association with me. John Lair had hired him to decorate an assembly room in a newly constructed broadcasting studio at Renfro Valley with a frieze of musician figures. In addition, his design for the Vicksburg, Mississippi, competition won him a commission for a small mural in the Campbellsville, Kentucky, post office. I was surprised at this because I felt that Bert's work still lacked a lot to be truly professional.

It seemed a long wait for a decision by the local committee and final approval by the Section of my design as the winner. The Section also had to approve my proposal to paint directly on the post office wall. I would have preferred to do this in all my murals, but from my standpoint it had never before been practical. The cost of having to take up residence at the mural location until the work could be finished would have been prohibitive, except in the case of my first government mural, in Lexington, since I could have lived there with my parents. However, in that case the fact that the wall was not suitable as a base for direct painting ruled out the possibility. I was pleased that here was an opportunity to paint in egg tempera with colors that I ground myself and mixed with the yolk of fresh eggs every working day. This is possibly the most permanent of all mediums for mural painting except true fresco, which is executed on damp plaster. There was no difficulty getting approval from the Section for this technique. Its permanence can be explained to the layman by citing the difficulty of removing well-dried egg yolk from the breakfast dishes.

One thing disturbed me greatly; Bert became almost openly hostile toward me after the award of the contract. He would barely speak when we passed each other. He must have felt that his design was superior to mine and was terribly disappointed that it did not win. More than that, I was told he confided to others he thought my design was chosen only because of Mary Ela's friendship with me. I had no idea up until then that he really felt his work was equal or superior to mine and was jealous of my success. Apparently this meant the end of our long friendship as far as he was concerned. I considered the loss a very great one, and it affected me deeply.

I thought of the many favors he had done for me, particularly during the period just after I completed the murals for the University of Kentucky library in the studio he had found for me and that we occupied together. This was a difficult time of adjustment for me, and he helped in more ways than one. I began to wonder if this had been only because he felt dependent on my ability to provide the instruction he needed to improve his artistic ability. It was a very disturbing question to consider.

I went to work almost immediately on a scaled-up working sketch to be used for reference while working on the wall. I made still larger drawings of some of the more important figures for reference also. In all the preparation required, including the building of a scaffold to work from in the lobby, I had planned to utilize Alonzo's help as usual. To my chagrin, before I began Alonzo came to tell me he had made a trip to Dayton, Ohio, and had taken a job there in a plant involved in some phase of the auto industry. He seemed as sorry as I was that our working together was to come to an end, at least for the moment, but hoped it might resume some time. Naturally, he was elated to have landed a job in spite of his criminal record and at the prospect of making a good deal more money than I was able to pay him. I was glad for his sake too.

Fortunately, I was able to get Chester Parks to take Alonzo's place. He was a very good carpenter, and we soon had the scaffold in place. It was built around the door to the postmaster's office and allowed easy access thereto. We then applied the paper for the cartoon to one of the long walls of the studio so that I could begin drawing the complete design at full scale in preparation for perforating the outlines on the post office wall in the usual manner. When this was finished, I asked Mary Ela to have a look and give her opinion of this stage of the work.

She expressed herself as being delighted and suggested I hold an open house, inviting the community to come have a look. I agreed with the idea, and I went back to work on the cartoon, shading the forms and figures to give a more complete conception, in black and white, of how the finished mural would look. I though that if some oldsters who could remember the event should attend they might call attention to anything out of harmony that I had included, or something I omitted that should have been shown.

In *Depression Post Office Murals and Southern Culture*, Beckham quotes a statement by Mary Ela:

I wish that you could have looked into Frank Long's studio last weekend and have seen the citizens of Berea viewing the cartoon for the Post Office mural. He invited them in on Saturday and Sunday, and they came in such crowds that it was as much as one's life was worth to see the "crowds at old time commencement" without a pretty emphatic foreground of contemporary Bereans. Mr. Long was generous in his explanation of procedures, and patient in his acceptance of criticism.

Someone suggested that I include more babies, and I think I agreed to try, but when I studied the design I could find no way to fulfill this request. This simply bears out my contention that a well-conceived design cannot be added to or subtracted from materially. If changes must be made, a whole new design is usually required, even though it might contain the same features. But my criticism of the mural remains: the panorama of the gathering should have contained many more elements. This would have created a better impression of what must have been a very crowded scene at its height.

In creating the various types of people to represent the crowd, I conceived the idea of using existing individuals as models for some of the figures. I did not have them pose, so it was a surprise when the resemblances were called to their attention by friends. I used Johnnie Niles as a young dulcimer player serenading his girlfriend in one corner of the foreground. Some others were Bereans who it seemed were easily recognized. I was accused of portraying myself in a character with a moustache like one I wore when I first came to Berea, but if there was a resemblance it was unintentional.

The week after the open house, Chester and I prepared the wall and transferred the lines of the cartoon to it in the usual manner. I then began the painting. My usual procedure was to work several hours a day. There was always a changing group of interested spectators as patrons of the post office came and went. I remember that I was bothered very little by questions or comments; everyone seemed to realize the importance to an artist of being allowed to concentrate, which I thought rather surprising.

I do not remember how long finishing the mural took, but I do recall one of Mary Ela's stipulations on accepting the appointment to chair the local selection committee. It was that an exhibition of examples of the winning artist's work would be shown in the college's art gallery. The Section of course had no objection; in fact, the staff there praised the idea. This exhibition took place while I was still working on the mural. I had on hand what I considered some good examples of my easel paintings, most of them recent, as well as some prints and drawings, and I felt very satisfied with the show when it was hung. It was perhaps no coincidence that the Section chose this particular time to send one of its personnel to inspect the progress of my work on the mural.

Olin Dows arrived late one afternoon. I met him at the bus station, and we went to dinner at the Colonial Hotel in the west end of town, where he had reserved a room. We had a long conversation after dinner. We discovered several common interests, one of which was an admiration for Thomas Wolfe's writing. To my amazement he revealed that he and Wolfe had attended Harvard together and were close friends. Still more amazing was the revelation that Dows was, in fact, the Joel Pierce in *Of Time and the River*. I knew then that he was the scion of the very wealthy, socialite family represented by the Pierces in the book. I was particularly surprised at his telling me this because Wolfe, although he treated their association as one of warm friendship, had expressed little respect for Pierce as an artist. Also, he was a little less than kind in his description of Pierce's (Dows's) mother. It seemed that Dows was either insensitive to the attitudes of others toward himself and his family, or that he had made up his mind to overcome any hurt he felt by boldly facing it.

The next morning, after he had viewed the mural and said he found it "most interesting" in its unfinished state, Dows wanted to see the exhibition in the art building gallery. He spent what I thought was a flattering amount of time viewing it. It was not until he left that I discovered he had bought two of the paintings. One of these was called *The Waiter*, a painting of a man impatiently waiting for his "date" to appear in the living room. The other was *Burnt Out*, the painting of the family described in the previous chapter. Dows had donated the first to the Berea College collection. I had no idea what he intended to do with the other.

It was a good many years later that I found out. I had come down to Washington for a meeting of the staff of the Indian Arts and Crafts

Board of the Interior Department. (I was the representative of the board in Alaska at that time.) During lunch, the manager of the board asked if I knew one of my paintings was hanging in the office of Stewart Udall, the secretary of the interior. In astonishment I said I did not.

"What's it called?" I asked.

"*Burnt Out*," he answered.

I knew then that it was in the Smithsonian collection, one division of which is the National Museum of American Art. The institution has a practice of lending works from the collection when requested by top government officials for temporary decoration of their offices. So Dows probably had this donation in mind when he bought the painting. (The University of Kentucky was also able to borrow it for a retrospective exhibition of my work in its art gallery in late 1991.)

When the mural was finished, it was photographed by a *Louisville Courier-Journal* photographer, and a large, full-color reproduction of it was used to illustrate a feature article by Rena Niles for a Sunday edition of the paper. Among the notables who came to see the mural as a result was the publisher of the *Courier-Journal*, Barry Bingham, who was also a member of the Board of Trustees of Berea College. Naturally, I had to be pleased by the publicity and the attention the mural received, in spite of my reservations about its artistic quality.

I do not remember whether or not the Section was prompt in its payment to me for this mural. It usually was not, and I, like many other artists in their program, very often had to wait beyond the date specified in the contract for the money we all needed so much. I feel sure this was not a matter of policy, but simply administrative incompetence. Still, it was a serious fault in a program that I still thought was meant to assist those whose economic status was badly eroded by the Great Depression.

I believe that, overall, the Berea mural gave me more pleasure in its execution than any of my other murals. This is really not surprising. I was working with subject matter I was most directly interested in and knowledgeable about. Although the event depicted went back a few years, the subject did not violate my prejudice against attempting to re-create a historical event about which I could have no firsthand knowledge. I even knew a few of the still-living former participants. It was most gratifying to receive their approval of the finished work.

Although most of those who have commented about my work believe the Berea mural to be my best effort as a muralist, my own opinion is that this is generally based on the appeal of its subject rather than on its aesthetic quality. Although my first murals done under the PWAP program in the University of Kentucky library have a good many faults, I consider them superior in the latter respect to any of my other murals. But there is no disputing the fact that the Berea mural has meant more to the community for which it was created than have any of the others.

CHAPTER 13
I Make My Final Escape from Mural Painting

ALTHOUGH I HAD ENJOYED CREATING the Berea mural, I was relieved when it was finally finished and I could get back to concentrating on other work that I could enjoy on a different plane. I believe it was at about this time that I was doing some paintings of cats, which had had a great attraction for me from early childhood on. While studying the French language and French literature in Paris, I had become acquainted with the works of Charles Baudelaire. I practiced my French by memorizing some of his poems and reciting them aloud for my instructor, trying to master correct pronunciation. Among his *Fleurs du Mal* were several about the cats Baudelaire admired so extravagantly. These did not exactly inspire my paintings, but they did stimulate my interest in using mental images of felines as models. I thought rather highly of some of the paintings, most of which were eventually sold. I now know the location of only three.

It was during this period (sometime in 1941) that I received notice from the Section that I had been granted another "also-ran" commission as a result of the St. Louis competition. This time I was genuinely astonished! I had thought so little of the sketches I submitted that I felt sure they would have no chance at any prize whatsoever. But I was somewhat encouraged by the location of the mural I was offered for the half-hearted effort I had made.

The mural was to be a panel in the Crawfordsville, Indiana, post office of about the same size as the Berea mural. I was considerably more familiar with that state than I had been with most of the other states in which I had competed for or won mural commissions. Both of my parents were natives of Indiana, and I had inherited several relatives who were still located there. My only sibling, Joe, was born in Indiana, and it was only due to better professional opportunities for my father that my parents had moved to Knoxville, Tennessee, a few years before I was born. Later, after my parents had moved to Kentucky, my mother and I often visited her brother's family in New

Albany, Indiana, just across the Ohio River from Louisville, during my vacations from art school. By a mild coincidence, my sweetheart from my high school days in Knoxville had moved with her family to the Indiana town of Evansville just after her graduation. Evansville is just over a hundred miles southwest of New Albany, and I managed to take advantage of this "relative" proximity to visit the object of my tender emotion whenever Mother and I were at my uncle's home. I would go down by bus, setting a time agreeable to my mother for my return, usually a week later. My girl's family seemed very patient about my periodic invasion of their privacy, which I'm afraid I was very casual about. I have an idea now that they were possibly thinking I might eventually take the responsibility of their daughter off their hands.

I shall always remember in some detail one of the trips I made to visit the young lady at that time. On that occasion I bought a round-trip ticket to take advantage of the slight reduction in cost. This proved to be a serious mistake, because I somehow managed to lose the return half of the ticket, discovering the loss just before the time for my return to New Albany. The worst of the situation was that I had spent all the remaining money I had after buying the ticket on entertaining my girl and myself.

In those early days of my youth I was very sensitive about my mistakes, especially where my girl and her family were concerned. I could not even consider admitting the loss and appealing to them to help me out of my financial difficulty with a small loan. I thought a little "innocent" lie was much to be preferred. I said I had decided to hike at least part of the way to New Albany because I was anxious to get an idea of the landscape of that part of Indiana. I was sure the family thought I was just a crazy artist anyway, and would accept this explanation without question—which of course they did. There was another element in the situation that made speed a factor; I had set the date for my return with my mother, and I simply had to return to New Albany on time to keep her from worrying and trying to get in touch with me in Evansville, as I knew she would do if I did not appear on schedule.

I had wangled a road map from a filling station, and I saw I could cut a great many miles off my journey by following a new highway under construction that cut through farmland and a few wooded areas. This was being built specifically to shorten the route from east to west. There would be no traffic on it except for construction crews and their heavy equipment, so no hitchhiking opportunities would be available. Anyhow, in those days hitchhiking had not yet developed the popularity it enjoyed a few years later when there was more auto traffic. But I was sure I could save a good deal of time by hiking this rough route across many miles to where it joined the old highway not far from New Albany. I was persuaded to try it by the thought that I could travel the distance in the two days available if I walked steadily, and rapidly, for ten or twelve hours a day. I was also influenced by the fact that there was no other way I could possibly do it.

I started the next morning just at daylight without disturbing anyone. I made some kind of sandwich, taking it and an apple for my breakfast somewhere along my route. I wrapped these and my few belongings—toilet articles and a change of underwear that I had brought with me—in a large bandanna. This made a small packet that I tied and slung over my shoulder with a strong cord. I was not long in reaching the beginning of the new highway and getting onto the graded roadbed. It was a little rough, of course, but not enough to slow my brisk pace. I figured that I had at least two or three hours before any work on the road would begin. As I was passing a point where much of the heavy road equipment was waiting the arrival of the road crews, the sun appeared just above the horizon. I remember well the enchanted scene the sunlight created in striking the mud-covered machinery at a low angle and turning it all to solid gold.

At some point when I began to feel hungry I stopped, sat on the side of the road on a boulder, and consumed the sandwich and the apple. I had become just a little tired, momentarily, and this small amount of food gave me renewed energy. I estimated I had covered about ten miles and was encouraged by the rate of speed I had been able to maintain. I enjoyed the scenery and being able to study the kinds of activity taking place in this part of the country. I had seen primarily agricultural land, consisting mostly of truck farms of vegetables with a spot or two of tobacco. Also, I could see that a lot of hogs were being raised. From time to time I would pass people working in the fields, and they would always respond to my waving while looking surprised at my presence. I saw a few cows and horses in the fields.

They are always part of the scene in farm country, which did not vary along the entire route.

From the position of the sun (I did not have a watch) I judged it to be about noon when I saw in the distance, off my path on a wandering side road, a little country store. I assumed the cluster of houses scattered around it represented a small, isolated community not far from a larger town that I could discern in the further distance. I hiked across open country and had to climb over a fence to reach the store. A few people seated on the porch watched my approach. None said a word of greeting when I climbed the steps and entered the store. I had exactly fifteen cents in my pocket. I hoped this would buy some cheese and crackers and a bottle of pop, which it did. I shall never forget the unexpected burst of restored energy this scant refreshment sent coursing through my entire body a few moments after I had consumed the last bite.

It is marvelous, the speed with which a healthy, youthful body recuperates. I was barely twenty and in excellent condition, having been in training for the track team at the Illinois Athletic Club in Chicago earlier that year. I was soon able to return to the roadbed and resume my steady, fast walking pace, covering almost as much distance in the afternoon as I had in the morning. Just before the sun sank and twilight began to spread over the landscape, I decided I had better find some sheltered spot where I could retire for the night. I was fairly exhausted, and I knew it would be dangerous to continue to walk in that condition, then try to find a stopping place in the dark.

A little further on, I saw a farmhouse not far off my route, and a farmer with a rake in hand standing near the big barn behind the house. I climbed the fence just off the shoulder of the road and walked across a field to where he stood. He seemed to eye my approach rather skeptically, but he wasn't unfriendly when I spoke and asked if I might sleep in his barn overnight. (I had to laugh when I thought of the title to a popular sentimental song of the period, "May I Sleep in Your Barn Tonight, Mister?") He asked a few questions that brought out the facts of my journey. I suppose the most important question from his standpoint was whether I smoked and had matches with me. Apparently he believed me, for he said I could sleep in the hayloft in the barn. He then pointed out the outdoor privy at some distance behind the house and a well nearby, tacitly suggesting I might find a use for both.

I remember how typical he was of the way everyone seemed to think a farmer should look: he wore blue overalls, a blue denim shirt, a straw hat, and a red bandanna around his neck. The only thing he lacked was the stem of a hayseed clamped between his teeth. I felt I shouldn't find fault with him—he was my host, if not overly gracious.

I thought it rather strange that I was not ravenously hungry as I made myself comfortable in the sweet-smelling hay in the loft. I suppose I was too tired to think about it, and I fell asleep almost immediately.

I awoke the next morning just as dawn was breaking. My muscles were a little sore, and I found I had made a bad mistake in taking my shoes off the night before. My feet were so swollen I had a very hard struggle getting them on again. I had some painful walking when I began, and it took some time before I was able to hit my fast stride and begin to cover ground at a satisfactory rate. Several hours later my route took me fairly near an apple orchard, and I climbed a fence and helped myself at the nearest tree. I have no idea now how many of the delicious winesaps I ate as I rested. I could see a house at no great distance from the orchard, but not a soul was in sight as I rested and ate my fill. When I left I added several apples to my packet. I decided to save these until I was really hungry again.

The unfinished highway I was traveling ended just a few miles to the west of Corydon. It was almost dark when I could see the town not far in the distance. I knew that it was less than twenty miles from New Albany. I also knew that I was simply "out of gas" and could not walk that far. What was I to do? In situations of crisis like this it seems the mind is unusually resourceful. I remembered that my uncle, a prominent doctor whom everyone knew, or knew about, in that area, had once mentioned the owner of the Corydon bus station as a longtime friend from earlier days. I decided at once to ask him to help me with the modest cost of a bus ticket to New Albany. I promised to send repayment within a few days. He apparently believed my story—I imagine he was afraid of running the risk of not believing it if it was true, thus failing to do his friend, my uncle, a rather small favor.

I arrived in New Albany at almost midnight, having had to wait for the bus for what seemed to me an eternity. Still, it was better that

I arrived after dark. Everyone at my uncle's house had retired. The front door was unlocked (hardly anyone bothered to lock doors in that law-abiding era), and I entered noiselessly and went to the room I had been occupying before I left for Evansville.

The next morning everyone was surprised to see me, of course, but I simply explained that I had left Evansville late, though a day earlier than I had planned, because I wanted to be sure of arriving on time as promised.

The only excuse I have for including this rather long-winded story here is that it explains why I approached the mural in Crawfordsville with a little more enthusiasm than I did some others. The experience gave me a brief acquaintance with the rural life and the people of that area. During my walk, I kept thinking that this was the region where my parents had originated and that their early life must have been quite similar to what I was seeing of that of the few people along my route.

Although Crawfordsville is not in the area I had traveled, the surroundings were much the same in that region. Most of Indiana is agricultural, except where industry takes over in the far north. I find it significant that the influence of this experience on some of my earliest paintings is apparent, and of course I was thinking of it when I went to work designing the mural for Crawfordsville almost immediately after receiving the award. I decided on a composite farm scene with a number of figures and other elements arranged arbitrarily within the approximately eight-by-twenty-foot panel. These represented agriculture and stock farming. Of course their treatment was symbolic rather than realistic. I was fairly pleased with the result, which passed the Section's jury without any comment, leaving me free to go ahead with my work on the canvas itself.

Although I no longer had an assistant to help with the preliminary preparation, I was not too long in finishing that part of the project alone. As I remember, I did take more time than usual on this project as a whole, however. I was more interested in the subject than I had been in most others, and there was no deadline pressing me. Because of the local interest in my work, generated by the Berea post office mural, I had visitors almost every day to watch the progress I was making. I was flattered rather than disturbed by this show of community interest in my career as a painter, even though I was not

Indiana Agriculture, *Crawfordsville, Indiana.*
Courtesy National Archives.

Detail from Indiana Agriculture.

primarily a muralist. I felt the interest extended, in some degree at least, to my other, more personal and more deserving work.

The approval of my sketch and the signing of the contract for this mural were not accomplished until late in 1941. This was a period of great stress in America. The rise of Hitler in Germany and his domination of western Europe during the last several years of the 1930s had alerted many in the United States to the danger this megalomaniac posed for the rest of the world, including their own country. This was not a real source of anxiety for Berea's public as a whole, but there were at least several members of the college faculty who thought about it seriously. It concerned me too, but I was not greatly disturbed by it; my mind was on more immediate concerns. However, the Japanese attack on Pearl Harbor, on December 7 of that year, shattered any complacency I may have had, as it did that of the entire nation. We were now at war with Japan and were almost certain to become embroiled in Europe against Hitler's conquest.

Our defense department was not long in inaugurating a national conscription act. I did not think this would affect me, personally, feeling vaguely that at thirty-six I would be too old for the draft. But I began to feel a patriotic obligation to help, if I could, any effort to rid our country of a dire threat to its security. The perfidy of the Japanese and the cynical decimation of entire ethnic populations by Hitler affected me deeply. I was both surprised and stimulated by the possibility that I might be called into military service; then I received a notice early in 1942 to appear before the local draft board and explain any reason I should not be called to serve. I was sure I would be excused if I would explain that I was supporting my aged mother, although if the case were investigated it would probably be concluded that my brother could replace me in this capacity if necessary. He had his own immediate family to care for, of course, but his financial condition would have allowed him to assume this additional responsibility.

The more I thought about it, however, the more I felt obligated. And there was another factor I was more than willing to consider. Any perceptive reader of this account of my dependence on government subsidy for the murals I had been engaged in painting can see that I was almost at the desperation point in my desire to escape from a situation that I disliked intensely—and even considered less than honorable. I knew that giving up my career as a muralist would be a genuine relief, no matter what else happened. At last I decided to let the draft board know that I would rather enlist than be drafted. I had found that certain subtle advantages were available to the enlistee in a case like mine. I also found that the age limit to be drafted was thirty-eight at that time, and I thought my desire to serve at my age was apt to be considered a point in my favor.

I was still working on the Crawfordsville mural. Since this was a government contract, I felt sure I would have no trouble obtaining deferral by the draft board until it was finished—and this was exactly what happened when I made the request. I was also surprised and gratified to learn that my mother would be granted a forty-dollar-per-month subsistence allowance as long as I should be in the service. No mention was made of my brother's ability to help financially.

I actually felt a flood of relief when this was all settled. I had no idea how I could support myself if I should return from the war in an able-bodied condition; I only knew I would never again try to depend on a career as an artist for my sole support. I was sure I could find some other agreeable employment, hopefully something allowing me some time to resume and continue painting, which I felt compelled to do. I was an eternal optimist, and that philosophy served me well in this instance.

The draft board had merely asked how long I expected to be involved in finishing the mural. Since there was no deadline set by the Section, I gave myself adequate time, both to finish the mural and to deal with the personal loose ends I would have to tie up. I did want to get through with everything without rushing. I had to alert my brother to the situation, of course, so that he would be prepared for any emergency that might arise. In discussing the situation with Mother, I found that she was quite willing to remain in Berea in the apartment over the bank. Although she would miss me deeply, like any mother whose son goes off to war, she was as philosophical as I was about my duty to serve my country. But bless her, I knew how difficult it was for her to face such a loss, particularly at her age.

When at last the mural was finished, I had to find someone to accompany me to Crawfordsville and help with the installation. It was during my last trip to Lexington to let my friends there know of my imminent departure from Kentucky that this problem was solved. In talking to Ted Rannalls about my need for an assistant, I was overwhelmed with surprise when he volunteered for the job. He was on a yearlong sabbatical from the university, so he had the time, he said. He had always expressed great interest in my work, and we had developed a very warm friendship, but I thought it a bit out of character for the head of a university art department to engage in this kind of labor. I had to believe that he simply wanted to provide the help he thought I needed. I tried to convince him that my need was not really that serious—that I knew I could find the help with no great trouble—but he persisted, and the matter was settled. I cannot recall the details of the trip or the installation, probably because there were no difficulties involved. Ted was more than adequate as a helper.

I do remember that the postmaster was very interested in the procedure we used in attaching the canvas to the wall with white lead paste, and that he seemed highly pleased with the mural. I was rather pleased with it myself, in contrast with some of my other murals.

Before leaving Berea for better or worse, among my preparations was the need to see to selling my car. There was not time enough to do this myself, so I left the transaction in the hands of Bill Mallicote, who owned the gas station I patronized the most. He was very accommodating and took on the task without a fee. I had perfect confidence in his honesty and arranged for him to remit the proceeds to my mother.

A more serious problem was what to do with my three beagle hounds. I finally arranged for Tom Bradford, one of the hunters I knew in Rockcastle County, to keep them for me until my return— or until it was certain I would never return, in which case he was to become the owner. For me, leaving them was almost as sad a parting as saying good-bye to my mother.

No matter how much longer I may live, I shall never forget my last sight of those three little hounds, sitting where I had ordered them to stay, with their new master in front of his little cabin. When I stopped a short distance down the path to my car and turned for a last look, they raised their muzzles skyward and, in perfect unison, gave tongue to the sadness of parting with the most piteous howls anyone has ever heard.

I never saw any of the three little hounds again. When I returned from the army, nearly four years later, and drove out to Tom's cabin, he told me how Jack had fallen over dead while he was hunting with him, probably from a heart attack. Jason had simply disappeared while on a chase alone. A thorough search over a large surrounding area failed to find any sign of him. As for Molly, Tom was sure she had been stolen by a foxhunter who lived in a very remote area in Clay County. There seemed no possibility of ever getting her back. I continue to grieve over my loss every time I think of the many happy days I enjoyed with those faithful little companions of the chase.

Finally, I needed to let all my friends know of my imminent departure. Among the closest of these were Arthur Rogers and his family. Arthur had become one of my hunting and fishing companions. He and his wife, Helen, had come to Berea from West Virginia some years before. They had five children, all girls, something of a disappointment to Arthur only because he had kept trying for a boy. He and his father operated a coal mine at some distance from Berea in Jackson County, but close enough that Arthur could drive to and from work. They were often involved in labor disputes with the miners' union and other mine owners. I had the greatest respect for Arthur, who in spite of all his difficulties in trying to provide for his big family, and his many other problems, was always ready to help others who faced the same or more serious difficulties.

There is not room in this chronicle to mention all the friends I made in Berea in the years of my sojourn there. I can only speak of some with whom I shared the experiences I have included here in the hope they may be of interest to my readers. One of these was Sam Farmer, who had become chief of police in Berea at the time of my departure. He and I had been hunting together a number of times, and when I decided to go on one last squirrel hunt, on my very last day before reporting for duty to my new employer, I asked Sam to accompany me. I always enjoyed Sam's company, especially for his highly original sense of humor. He could find something to laugh at in almost any situation—even those no one else thought funny until he brought the comic element to their attention. I had decided almost on the spur of the moment that I wanted to go on a last, brief afternoon hunt along Silver Creek where Sam's cousin, one of the numerous Maupin tribe, owned some property. I knew that several large, rusty-coated fox squirrels nested along the creek and wrought havoc in the cornfields of that area, but I enjoyed the environment of the creek even more, I believe, than I did the hunt itself.

Silver Creek ran near a section called the Glades on the northern edge of Berea and then passed on through the open fields of the farms in that area. It was bordered in most places by cottonwood, sycamore, and black walnut trees. It presented a quiet, sylvan, almost medieval aura, which excited the imagination and encouraged revery.

It was Sam's day off, but he had to take his wife to Purkey's store at the west end of Berea for something before he could leave. To save time I went with them in Sam's car and waited with him, parked outside, for her return. It was during this wait that I brought up a question that I had often thought about but had never discussed with anyone, as far as I can remember. It concerned the town of Berea's legal status as a community. I knew it had a mayor, but I could not remember any election being held for that office. Then there was the "prudential committee," which apparently decided with the mayor the policies and procedures concerning operation of the town. I knew that most of the members of this body were personnel of the college, but I was aware of one member who was an independent citizen. I am puzzled today to explain to myself why I was so woefully ignorant about this important element of the town's operation.

I do remember well that the consensus was that the college ran the town. I had heard that no one could start a business in Berea without the college's approval. An example was cited of one of the large chain grocery companies having made an unsuccessful attempt to locate one of their stores in Berea.

I also remember a startling occurrence that was never explained but seems to clearly indicate that the college had unlimited power to suppress public information in matters involving the college. One fine evening a girl student was sitting on the steps of a campus building with several friends when another student approached, drew a pistol, and shot the girl dead. (The boy was the girl's rejected lover.) The murderer ran off in the dark. No one followed, and it seems that he was never seen or heard of again. Apparently, there was never any investigation, legal or otherwise, of this incident, and never a word about it appeared in any of the news media—local, state, or national. Unfortunately, I can give no date for this mournful drama; I only know that it occurred during the time I was occupying the studio on Main Street.

In the very short interval before Sam's wife reappeared, I asked Sam a few questions concerning these matters, and the subject was continued as we drove on toward the creek after leaving her at their home. I do not believe that Sam was intentionally evasive in his answers, and perhaps my memory at this late date is at fault, but I cannot remember that he was of much help in clearing up the uncertainty in my mind concerning these things. Recently I have asked these questions of both the present mayor of Berea and some of those who are still available among the old-timers. It seems that no one can remember a "prudential committee" or other details of the city administration of fifty years ago. Certainly it isn't surprising that everything has changed radically today, and no doubt for the better.

It was rather late in the day when Sam and I finally invaded the peaceful atmosphere of Silver Creek. We saw no squirrels as we slipped quietly along the banks of the creek at some distance from each other on opposite sides of the stream. But just as I had decided we might as well give up our hunt because it had become almost too dark to aim a rifle, I saw some movement in the foliage of a tree across the creek. The next instant a large squirrel appeared on a projecting limb, outlined against the sky. It had a nut of some kind in its paws. As it settled down to gnaw on the nut, I placed the crosshairs of my sight on its head and squeezed the trigger. The squirrel fell with a resounding plop on the creek bank. With the shot, Sam came along that side of the creek and picked up the dead squirrel. It was a large but young fox squirrel. As we walked out from under the trees with it, I was startled when I saw it in the light of the open sky. I had never seen a fox squirrel of that color. It was pure silver gray, with a bushy tail that was almost silver white; but its short ears, general conformation, and size identified it as unmistakably a fox squirrel. This species is considerably larger than the gray squirrels inhabiting the same area, and its fur is normally a rusty orange red color mixed with just a little gray on the back. I have an idea that if the light had been bright and I could have seen the animal's unique coloration I would have refrained from killing it. I have always had a prejudice against killing one of a kind of any species.

When I expressed this sentiment, Sam laughed and asked, "Well, Private Long, when you git into battle are ya gonna bother about knowin' if the man you shoot is only one of a kind or not?"

I had to admit he had a point. In fact, later I began to think about it seriously and I had to question whether, if I were faced with having to kill another human being, I could pull the trigger. With humans of any color, every one is unique and should be allowed every possible chance to live. I supposed it might be different if I should be faced with a choice between killing or being killed. Still, Sam's words made me understand the problem every conscientious objector faces in time of war. These were disturbing thoughts that many soldiers have, but which I had never properly considered before. When we parted, I gave the squirrel to Sam along with my final farewell till we should meet again.

The next day my mother and I said our good-byes. She was smiling through her tears, and I had to kiss her quickly to control mine. A group of several friends saw me off at the Berea railroad station, where I boarded a train for Covington, Kentucky. From there I reported to the induction center at Fort Thomas, near Covington, where I was duly sworn in to serve in the army of the United States of America for the duration of the war, thus terminating my ten-year career as an artist and mural painter in Berea, Kentucky.

Tomorrow I would feel like a reptile must feel when it has shed an old skin that has become so uncomfortable it has to be rid of it. Everything would be new and different. I would be surrounded by strangers. Most would be a great deal younger than I was. Would I be able to keep pace with them in adjusting to a totally new life? Then the blind optimism that had always served me in times of stress took control. I turned over on the strange barracks cot, pulled the blanket around my shoulders, and went soundly to sleep knowing that I would.

Afterword

Harriet W. Fowler

FOLLOWING FRANK LONG'S INDUCTION into the U.S. Army, he was assigned to the 603d Camouflage Battalion of the Corps of Engineers at Fort Mead, Maryland. He had specifically requested the assignment, hoping that his artistic talents might be applicable to the camouflage battalion and also because Laura Whitis was working for the War Department in nearby Washington, D.C. The day after he finished basic training, he was made a private first class, and he and Laura were married in the First Christian Church on Dupont Circle in Washington. Promoted through the grades to technical sergeant, he was assigned to the Officer's Candidate School at Fort Belvoir, Virginia; after seventeen weeks of training he was commissioned a second lieutenant in the Corps of Engineers. He then served in the Pacific Theater of Operations until 1946, finishing his tour of duty in North Korea by helping deport the Japanese. Discharged on May 18, 1943, he traveled with Laura from the separation center at Camp Beale, California, to Berea, Kentucky, where they bought eight acres of land three miles from town on the Scaffold Cane Road in Rollie Davis Hollow.

By this time the great federal programs of artistic patronage had ended, having shut down in 1943 as the United States geared up for entry into World War II. Long realized he must find a way of making a living other than by painting and took advantage of the G.I. Bill of Rights. He and Laura traveled to what was then New Mexico State Teachers College at Silver City, where he studied for a year in the art department, learning leatherwork, lapidary techniques, silversmithing, and jewelry design. In 1947, at the end of the school year, the Longs returned to Berea and built a rammed-earth house (which still stands), a workshop, and a studio in Rollie Davis Hollow.

At this time the artist started his own business of producing and selling original contemporary jewelry, largely one-of-a-kind designs. He joined the Southern Highlands Handicraft Guild and participated in its workshops, exhibitions, and arts and crafts fairs. In 1951, just as the couple was starting to make a living from the sale of his work, the Indian Arts and Crafts Board, a federal agency under the Interior Department, offered him a position as its field representative in Alaska. The artist accepted the job, recognizing the position as a good opportunity to further develop his lapidary and jewelry-making skills while enjoying the adventures of living in Alaska with new cultures of people. He and Laura moved to Juneau, the capital of Alaska, so Long could travel throughout the Territory (as it was then) setting up production workshops for Alaskan Eskimos and Indians.

In 1953 a daughter, Angela Elaine, was born. The harsh northern climate may have been too difficult for this child, who had respiratory problems from birth. Responding to the doctor's opinion that Angela needed sunshine and warmth to get well, in 1958 Long requested a transfer to a post in the Southwest. The result was a move to Gallup, New Mexico, where Long's district centered in the southwestern states. During his service as field representative for the board, he worked with all the tribes in the area, advising them on the production and distribution of their arts and crafts products. He also acted as liaison between Indian tribes and agencies of the government that could provide funds for development work.

The pull of Kentucky and the Appalachians was strong, however, and in 1959 Long resigned his position with the board and returned to Kentucky to reopen his jewelry business. One year later he was recalled by the board (now titled the Bureau of Indian Affairs) for a special assignment—that of assisting the Seminole Tribe at Dania, Florida, in organizing an arts and crafts enterprise. He accepted the assignment, perhaps because the winter of 1959 had been one of Kentucky's most severe and Angela had reacted poorly to the sudden change from the warm southwest. After completing the project in eighteen months, in 1962 Long accepted reassignment by the board to the southwest, reopening his office in Albuquerque. He remained with the board until his retirement in 1969, organizing several crafts cooperatives including the successful Zuni Craftsmen's Association in New Mexico and the Hopi Silvercraft and Arts and Crafts Guild in Arizona. His retirement coincided with the closing of the board's field offices and its recentralization in Washington, D.C.

New leisure allowed the pursuit of his artistic projects full-time. In 1977 Van Nostrand Reinhold Company published his book *The Creative Lapidary*, which detailed his knowledge of metal crafts and lapidary techniques. Long was an active crafts exhibitor throughout the 1960s and 1970s, with his work represented at national exhibitions at the Everhart Museum in Scranton, Pennsylvania, in 1963; the Southwest Crafts Biennial in 1963 at the Museum of International Folk Art in Santa Fe, New Mexico; the New York World's Fair New Mexico Exhibit of 1965; the National Invitational Crafts Exhibition held at the University of New Mexico Gallery in 1968; the New Mexico Crafts Biennial at the Museum of National Folk Art in 1974; the Southwest Crafts Biennial at that same institution the following year; and the Crafts V and Crafts VII exhibitions at the Museum of Albuquerque in 1973 and 1977. Most recently he was the subject of a 1991 retrospective at the University of Kentucky Art Museum in Lexington, Kentucky; the exhibition featured works from his entire career, including mural sketches, paintings, prints, and jewelry.

In recent years the artist has dedicated his energy to his first great interest: easel painting. Compelled by economic necessity at the beginning of his career to concentrate on murals and then, for most of his life, to focus on crafts, he has now returned to that first love. The late oil paintings, which date from the 1980s, offer a fascinating synthesis of artistic knowledge gleaned over a lifetime. The rugged landscapes and sturdy people and animals of the 1930s and 1940s have been transformed into complex geometric forms, their monochromatic color harmonies now higher keyed, brilliantly saturated. Yet, like those earlier works, they reveal a joyous harmony with the universe and the subtle, nervous energy and rhythmic grace that are uniquely Frank Long's own.